CREATING SPIRITUALLY INSPIRED PROJECTS

By

Barry Taylor

Creating Spirituality Inspired Projects

Published by New Generation Publishing in 2015

Copyright © Barry Taylor 2015

First Edition

The author asserts the moral right under the Copyright, Designs and Patents Act 1988 to be identified as the author of this work.

All Rights reserved. No part of this publication may be reproduced, stored in a retrieval system or transmitted, in any form or by any means without the prior consent of the author, nor be otherwise circulated in any form of binding or cover other than that which it is published and without a similar condition being imposed on the subsequent purchaser.

ISBN 978-1-78507-208-6

www.newgeneration-publishing.com

Creating Spirituality Inspired Projects

*Available from all major book stores including
Waterstones and Amazon*

*To get in touch with the author, visit his website at
www.savaric.com*

Contents

Introduction 1
A Spiritual World 5
    Spiritual Teachers 7
    Wisdom 18
    Practice 27
    The Journey 33
    Guidance 39
Spiritual Projects 47
    Glastonbury 48
    Balance 57
    Conception 63
    Birth 73
    Maturity 85
    Apparent 'Problems' 90
    Conclusion 99
APPENDICES 102
Appendix1 - Wisdom 103
Appendix 2 - Glastonbury 109

Creating Spirituality Inspired Projects

*Dedicated to my colleagues in Glastonbury
and the concept of Stewardship*

Creating Spirituality Inspired Projects

Introduction

I started my working life in the conventional worlds of business, finance and charity. In 1985 I was 'called' to Glastonbury and started regularly visiting. In 1990 I came to live here.

Whilst living in Glastonbury, my work has continued with charities, but now with those that are unconventional and involve some form of 'spiritual inspiration'.

In thinking about these two halves of my life, I was intrigued by the similarity between the working processes of the conventional world and Glastonbury, but also the subtle differences. The traditional methods of achieving material success are clearly understood and taught by the business schools. Spiritually inspired projects require slightly different methods. The practical approach of the business world is needed, but with the addition of the inspiration of the spirit world. This calls for the delicate balancing act of walking between two extremes – spiritual inspiration and material reality.

There appear to be few books on establishing and running a community project inspired by the spirit, and I felt that writing something on this subject would be worthwhile.

So, how best to do this? The ideas I wish to explore are not comprehensible without some understanding of the town of Glastonbury and the concept of spiritual inspiration. Glastonbury has a recorded history, but the aspect of the town leading to spiritual inspiration can only be experienced. Similarly, the whole concept of the spirit is not open to factual proof. Numerous books are available on the spiritual world, but in every case what is being described is subjective and individual – a unique experience not repeatable by others.

A factual textbook cannot be written about spiritual inspiration! The only practical alternative seems to be to write in a personal manner. I have gained some useful practical experience whilst working with these unusual projects and this is the basis of this book. Everything contained here is one person's subjective understanding of this type of activity, and the world of the Spirit, as found in the town of Glastonbury in Somerset, England. Other readers may have different views but I ask you to hold what I have to say as a hypothesis that may have value and could be a useful start for further exploration. The phenomenon experienced in this town will also exist in other towns where the numinous energy is strong. The process may be different but the pattern will be similar.

In order to achieve a sustainable level of material well-being for all, we need to create balance and harmony between a scientific approach of cold, calculating action and a spiritual, intuitive and inspired way of working. This difficult balancing act, esoterically called the 'Razor's Edge', means working with two essential but contradictory themes. This is the fascinating paradox we will be exploring in this book.

Working with projects of this type is rewarding. Progress is often slow, with many disappointments and apparent failures, but in the end, if the concept is genuinely spiritually inspired, something wonderful will emerge. The result may not be what was first envisaged, but it will be worthwhile in whatever final form it takes.

I have used the personal pronoun 'he' and the possessive pronoun 'his' instead of endless repetition of 'he/she' or 'his/her'. There is no gender preference in the work in which we are concerned.

The reader wishing to explore these ideas further will find a wealth of information on the Internet. This research may also lead to some useful intuitive and synchronistic hints. Often, in researching one facet, an interesting name or thought appears, which, in turn leads to further discoveries.

May all who read this book enjoy the experience and fulfilment that goes with working with this extraordinary process.

Barry Taylor
Glastonbury
2015

Creating Spirituality Inspired Projects

Creating Spirituality Inspired Projects

A Spiritual World

Spiritual Teachers

Before we explore inspired projects, an understanding of what we mean by spirituality is needed.

From our position in the early 21st century, spirituality appears to be an ill-defined area of human experience not verifiable by current scientific means. Nevertheless, whilst not provable by today's standards, it has been directly experienced, written and talked about by thousands of individuals over millennia.

The difficulty of studying the subject is compounded by the wide variety of interpretations of the meaning of spirituality. But if we look at the writings of mystics and teaching of the ancient Mystery Schools we see an underlying eternal and universal truth. This eternal truth has many names, including the 'Perennial Philosophy' and the 'Ageless Wisdom'. Understanding this teaching is the essence of grasping the concept of a world of the spirit. We will start by looking at the proponents of this idea of Ageless Wisdom and in the next chapter look at the teaching itself.

The first clear historical record of this eternal Wisdom is seen in the mystery schools of Egypt and Greece. These schools taught the 'Greater Mysteries', reserved for a select and trained few, and the 'Minor Mysteries' available to all.

The Greater Mysteries were held to be unsuitable for revelation to those not suitably trained. These secrets were for methods usable both for positive good and for evil, and in consequence, were only safe in the hands of those tested for their purity of purpose. The conditions for entry were strict and a vow of silence was imposed on every pupil, hence why few written records survive.

The Wisdom traditions led to the emergence of an understanding of an 'Esoteric' secret inner core to religions, confined to ordained priests and monks, containing the teaching of spiritual truths and practices and the concept of the Divine being directly accessible to the individual. The outer 'Exoteric' component contained ceremonies and parables suitable for illiterate and untrained minds. This outer teaching could lead to raising an individual's awareness, so enabling the comprehension of the inner spiritual essence of the faith.

The methods and practices of the mystery schools were not recorded, but clear indications of the teaching appear in the writings of the classical Greek philosophers. Plato defined human reality as having three components – the external material world, the internal world of the individual mind and the numinous, divine eternal world. With Plato, we see a clear definition in the historical records of what we will call the 'Wisdom'.

This teaching of the Greek philosophers was lost to Western Europe for years, and only emerged with its rediscovery in the early 16th century. Since then, Plato's thinking has been the foundation of much Western philosophical and spiritual understanding.

From this time on, the concept of the Wisdom begins to gather momentum and the term 'Philosophia Perennis' or 'Perennial Philosophy', appears in the early 16th century in the writings of Agostino Steuco. Later the idea was carried forward and expanded by Gottfried Leibnitz in a book, published in 1687. All such teachings were anathema to the Christian Church, holding as it did, that Christianity was the only true religion – the concept of the truth of Christianity being similar to other religions was not acceptable. The fear of persecution by the church led to the teachings of the Wisdom continuing, but remaining hidden.

In the 19th century, huge strides were made in the advance of science and understanding of nature. The steam engine was invented, and Charles Darwin published his book on the 'Origin of the Species'. This growth in awareness of how the material world appeared to operate led to an undermining of the acceptance of dogmatic religious beliefs and openness to other concepts of the spiritual world. Inspired by a renewed interest in the Greek philosophers and a feeling of freedom from the authority of the church, the thesis of the Wisdom re-emerged. Ralph Waldo Emerson established the 'Transcendentalist' movement and published a number of classic books, including *Self-Reliance* and *The Over-Soul*.

This new 'awakening' brought the idea of spirituality, independent of religion, into a new and respectable acceptance. These hypotheses were further elaborated and defined at the end of the 19th century, with the publication of various books by Helena Petrovna Blavatsky. She sought to teach that the same underlying principles lay behind not only Christian, but also Hindu and Buddhist traditions. She set up the Theosophical Society to promote her ideas, referring to them as 'Wisdom-Religion' and the 'Ancient Wisdom'. From this Society emerged the teachings of Annie Besant and a number of other streams of thought, including those of Rudolf Steiner (the Anthroposophical Society) and Jiddu Krishnamurti.

In the early 20th century, Alice Bailey left the Theosophical Society and set up her own organisation: the Lucis Trust. She wrote a number of books, channelling the words of an ascended master, Djwhal Kuhl, and used the term 'Ageless Wisdom' for her teaching.

These emerging schools reiterated the ancient concept that, provided certain spiritual disciplines were followed, the individual could make direct contact with the Divine, without the intermediary of priests and or the need to follow a specific religion.

The Wisdom teachings of these early exponents were complex, intellectual and not easy to understand and hence followed by only a small number of committed people. An exception was perhaps Rudolph Steiner who achieved wide acceptance amongst scientists and professionals.

In 1911, Evelyn Underhill's classic book *Mysticism* was published. There was little initial interest in the subject but this changed when, in 1945, the popular author, Aldous Huxley, published his book the *Perennial Philosophy*, within which he defined the eternal Wisdom and its origins.

In the early part of the 20th century, only a small number of people took an interest in these concepts. However, in the 1960s and 70s, the so-called 'Flower Power' and 'Hippy' movements emerged, bringing a growing awareness of 'New Age' philosophy reflecting the Wisdom.

So we begin to find the Wisdom bubbling up in new forms in numerous places and guises. Let us look at some of the specific ways in which it manifests.

Established Religion

In the West, the early part of the 20th century saw a gradual decline in the support for traditional religions. The exoteric side of these religions was losing support, but this was partially balanced by an increased interest in the esoteric side. The conventional churches mistrusted mystics for their perceived potential for disruption and mysticism was mainly confined to monasteries and books published by mystic writers. The increasing openness of the 20th and 21st centuries, and the availability of popular books on every conceivable esoteric subject, lead to a new interest in these aspects of the established churches, some of which are defined below:

Judaism - There is a growing interest in the Kabbalah, known in other teachings as the 'Tree of Life'. This is a collection of esoteric teachings explaining the relationship between the ever-changing material world and the unchanging, eternal and divine One, and exploring the relationship between the human and divine aspects in a classical Wisdom manner. Interest in the Kabbalah and the Tree of Life is now found far beyond the confines of the Jewish religion.

Christianity - Christian mysticism sees the ultimate purpose of the Christian life as union with Christ. Whilst this is the belief of mystics, it has not always been taught to members of Christian congregations. In recent years, a wider public has become aware of these beliefs through the writings of Christian monks, including Bede Griffiths and Thomas Merton. Their teaching follows the classical Wisdom in including the practices of meditation and contemplation as ways of enabling the individual to attune directly with the divine, and the acceptance of Christian meditation using a mantra or sacred phrase is becoming more widely accepted. Interest in Christian mysticism increased with the publication of the recently discovered Red Sea Scrolls and the gospel of St Thomas.

Islam - The classic form of Islamic mysticism is the Sufi tradition, made popular in the West through the teachings of Rumi. Sufism is held to be a science that enables the individual to attain the presence of the divine and thus purify the inner self. Once again, this tradition emphasizes the ability of the individual to approach the divine directly, without the necessity of an intermediary. Sufi beliefs have found a significant number of followers in the West during the last few years, and these people are not necessarily Islamic practitioners. An interesting aspect of contemporary spirituality is found in followers of the esoteric side of an established religion not always being practicing members of the exoteric side.

Buddhism - A number of Buddhist monks and teachers are practicing in the West. The Buddhist teaching of compassion, kindness and tranquillity as a path towards Nirvana has created a strong following, and the word 'mindfulness' is becoming part of everyday language. It is now an accepted practice for individuals, who are not overtly spiritually minded, to go on meditation retreats in Buddhist centres.

Hinduism - The Hindu tradition covers a range of practices leading to enlightenment and one-ness with the divine and has had a powerful influence on the emerging contemporary spiritual beliefs in the West, particularly in the writings of Mme Blavatsky and her followers. This faith is the basis for much of New Age philosophy, not only in theories of meditation but also in the practice of Yoga, now seen as a conventional secular exercise and practice.

Academia

The faculties of Comparative Religion in the universities are beginning to become aware of spirituality existing outside the established religions. The term 'Contemporary Spirituality' is now in use and various academics are investigating the subject and producing theses. This subject is difficult for academics, as individual spirituality is only understandable as a subjective experience and cannot be adequately described in a detached, objective manner. Some researchers are now writing two different versions of their findings – an academic, objective observation of the phenomena, and a separate paper on their own personal subjective experience.

Depth Psychology

Psychology purports to be a science. As such, it needs to study the mind and consciousness in a detached, objective fashion, which makes it difficult for the subjective experience of the client to be understood. This inherent problem led to deeper research into the unconscious and super-conscious. Sigmund Freud was the pioneer, followed by Carl Jung. More recent years have produced the full flowering of what is now called 'depth psychology', particularly in the work of Abraham Maslow and Roberto Assagioli. This new psychology accepts a personal Higher Self as being a part of a universal consciousness.

Conventional psychology still mistrusts the views of some of the depth psychologists.

New Age

The emerging spiritual awareness of the 1960s and 70s was then called the 'New Age'. This was not a specific spiritual path but rather an eclectic collection of beliefs, loosely based on aspects of Hindu mysticism, brought into public awareness by Mme Blavatsky and her colleagues. Over the years this expanded to include elements of Native American, Shamanic and early Celtic beliefs taken in different selections by individual centres and practitioners. Underlying these teachings, are the basic principles, which we have defined as being the Wisdom.

Recently, the all-embracing New Age concept has tended

to be replaced by specific contemporary spiritual paths, including the various branches of paganism.

The common denominator of these new belief systems is an understanding of spiritual awareness existing outside the established religions. With this goes a growing awareness of the many valid paths to the divine, the one to follow being a personal choice. This leads to an acceptance of the opinion that each of these paths is worthy of respect. This open-mindedness to other beliefs is a marked feature of New Age consciousness.

'Unity in Diversity' has emerged as an acceptable phrase in which this diversity is honoured. All paths are different and special in their own way, but all are a part of the divine One. The expression itself dates back centuries and was quoted by the Hindu Patanjali in the second century BC.

Mystery Schools

A number of new mystery schools are emerging, where the Wisdom is taught in various guises. Despite the huge amount of literature now in the public domain on the 'mysteries', there is still an element of secrecy about these contemporary schools. The key teachings are only revealed to those committed to going through the stages of 'initiation' as defined by the particular school. The underlying eternal concept remains – mastery of the mysteries leads to the ability to handle spiritual 'energies'. Understanding the use of these energies enables the practitioner to bring into being whatever the individual desires. Once acquired, these skills may be used for good or ill. The potential for misuse of this knowledge is the reason mystery schools keep such tight control of the teaching, as it is believed to be safe only to impart this understanding to individuals committed to the good and showing the ability to apply the necessary discipline.

There is a growing number of such schools, amongst the better known are: the Theosophical Society, Lucis Trust, and the Wrekin Trust in England, the Findhorn Foundation in Scotland and the Essalen Centre in California.

Pagan

The original meaning of the word Pagan was 'a villager or rustic'. More recently, it has come to mean a person who follows beliefs or practices outside the established religions.

Modern paganism takes many different forms, including Druidism, Wicca and the Goddess movement. The essential beliefs are to honour the spiritual nature of the landscape, the rhythm of the seasons and the non-human entities present in nature. This can be thought of as in contrast to the perceived view of Christianity, i.e. the worship of a single 'sky god' and contempt for the physical earth.

The term 'pagan' is taken to include the original cultures emanating from North America, Africa and Polynesia.

Few written records exist of these beliefs, which originate pre-Christianity. In the 20th century, these ancient pagan beliefs were rediscovered and defined and today they strike a chord with the modern sense of individuality and ecological awareness.

Scientific research

Some scientific research is being carried out into the spiritual world. The difficulty here is that science confines itself to the study of clearly recorded and repeatable phenomena, which does not allow it to accept subjective, intuitive ideas as valid. In consequence, phenomena are observed and commented upon without little real understanding of what is being experienced.

For this reason, most physical and biological scientists avoid any public suggestion of spiritual influence on material reality. Nonetheless, some scientists do privately consider science and spirituality to be complementary and recognition of this as being essential in order to interpret the physical world.

Self-help

Perhaps the most remarkable symptom of a growing spiritual awareness is the explosion of books, teachings, workshops and courses on what might be called 'Self-Help', whether these be the 12-step course of Alcoholics Anonymous, the original books of Norman Vincent Peale, or the multitude of books on 'how to stop smoking' and 'how to live a more satisfactory life'. Most of these are based upon aspects of the basic spiritual creative process discussed later in this book.

The situation in 2015

Many of the late 20th century teachers believed a new spiritual awareness was bursting upon the world leading to a universal understanding and acceptance of mysticism. If the tenets of the Wisdom were universally accepted then all would directly experience the Divine Truth and attitudes and behaviour would change accordingly. Sadly, with unrest, violence, distress, misery and uncertainty in so many parts of the world, this ideal situation is far from being realised and these views now appear to be rather naïve. There may not have been the anticipated growth in spiritual understanding, but there is hope in that some progress is being made in the growing awareness of ecology and human rights.

The galloping advance of pure materialism has many positive benefits, but this progress comes at a high price. We cannot but observe, whatever the cause, the climate changes leading to more violent storms, flooding and drought. With the feeling that nature is turning against us, has come the increasing disenchantment with the previously respected structures of banks, politicians, the services of the state, and even the established religions. Wherever we look, previously apparently sound systems are being shaken to their foundation.

Perhaps, the dying of the old will allow room for the new to be born, followed by a real step forward in human understanding, consciousness and compassion to the benefit of all living creatures and our precious earth. Maybe we are not far away from a new blossoming of the Wisdom and with it the beginnings of an understanding of how to achieve peace amongst the warring and divided peoples of the world.

Wisdom

Looking at the teachers of the Wisdom was straightforward as they are historically recorded and their existence can be taken as proven.

Now we need to study what was being taught. Here we are on the more difficult ground of subjective personal experiences of the spiritual world. They were describing something numinous and ephemeral that cannot be tested by conventional scientific means – indeed its very existence is today open to doubt.

To further confuse the situation, these ideas and thoughts are expressed in different ways and words, there being no universally accepted glossary of spiritual terms. Such is the breadth of views expressed that the descriptions might be of completely different things.

So in exploring the meaning of the Wisdom we will, for the purposes of this book, establish a few ground rules:

- Certain basic truths underlie the understanding of the spiritual world. These truths are universal and known by various terms including the Perennial Philosophy, and the Ageless Wisdom. We are calling these truths the Wisdom.
- There appear to be many different aspects to this truth, depending upon the culture, consciousness and awareness of the viewer.
- I will define the Wisdom, as I understand it. Others may see it differently, but one individual's view may be a helpful starting point.

So let us get on with our endeavour to define the Wisdom.

The Divine

The world of the Spirit is an all-embracing whole, with at its heart, all love, knowledge, truth, beauty, unity, harmony and compassion. The entire universe is a part of this one Whole, which is held together by the dynamic of love.

The whole material world is linked through this One and every action taken by an individual component affects the whole universe. The universal One revels in diversity as it creates new forms and levels of consciousness.

Unity in diversity is the very essence of the spiritual world.

The omniscience of this presence is described in the invocation, written by Annie Besant for the Theosophical Society:

'O Hidden Life! vibrant in every atom,

O Hidden Light! shining in every creature,

O Hidden Love! embracing all in Oneness,

May each who feels himself at one with Thee,

Know he is also one with every other.'

This One is accessible by the individual through practices, which enable the divine spark to be seen in all aspects of nature and other individuals. This applies to the arts, science, philosophy and religion, which can only be truly whole and complete, when accessing and honouring the numinous spiritual world.

This Divine presence has a purpose and guides humanity towards its fulfilment at a pace with which humanity is able to respond.

God

The word God is used by Christians to describe a Divine entity known by different names by other beliefs. This is the supreme intelligence holding the universe together and inter-penetrating every pattern and molecule of the material world. This universal One has three components:

God – the ground of being – the indescribable, infinite, eternal energy lying behind everything, and holding the whole universe together in a manner beyond the understanding of man.

God – the personal – the part of the infinite God able to understand and have compassion and love for all living creatures.

God – the communicating spirit – the aspect of the infinite God reaching out and communicating with mankind.

Grades of Divinity

A gulf exists between the consciousness of the Divine One and the awareness of a human being. Contemplating the extraordinary size and complexity of the universe, it is apparent that a mind capable of creating this whole is beyond human comprehension.

By necessity, a gradation of consciousness is needed between the one indescribable Divine and the ordinary human. This infinite ladder of consciousness – of different awareness and complexity – is occupied by intelligent entities from the most mundane to the most supreme. This range of beings, at different stages of consciousness, enables the incarnate human to find a guide at the level of awareness to which he can relate.

Spiritual Planes

The spiritual world is seen as occupying a number of different 'energy levels' or 'spiritual planes'. Use of words such as, 'energy' and 'levels', arises from an immaterial world being described with conventional material words. The spiritual concepts of energy and levels are not recognised by conventional science and in view of our lack of shared glossary we need to define how we are using these words in this context:

Energy – this is the concept of different spiritual and material entities vibrating at different 'frequencies', some of which are not currently measurable. This idea might be more acceptable if we think of the extraordinary spectrum of electromagnetic energy. Until recently, only a small section of this range of energy, visible light, was known. More has been learned with modern instruments, including X-rays and radio waves. Maybe one day, instruments will be developed able to record the currently undetectable spiritual energies.

Levels– the word 'levels' is used to describe different frequencies of spiritual energy. The words 'above' and 'below' are often used, and imply the physical separation of items that in reality occupy the same space, but at different energy levels. The spiritual world could be thought of as a different universe interpenetrating the physical world, in some ways analogous to the dozens of unseen television, radio and mobile signals flowing through the same place at the same time, but only observable with a suitable receiver.

These levels are described in many different ways, but the following is a working summary:

Spiritual Level – the level of pure spirit – the ground of all being.

Astral Level – sometimes called the **Akashic or Mind Level** – a non-material level, where the universal human emotions, feelings and thoughts are to be found. At this level are held what are called the Akashic Records – an accessible 'library' containing every thought, concept and idea that has ever been formulated.

The Etheric Level – a materially formless level of alive and intelligent energy: an energy permeating and filling the whole universe, being the raw material from which all physical objects are created. An idea, held firmly, with absolute clarity in this formless substance, creates a material copy on the Physical Plane.

The Physical Level – the material level at which all physical objects are found.

The Cosmic Plan

The Cosmos was created by an idea held at the Etheric level, which in turn brought into being the physical reality of the earth and the universe. There is a long-term plan for the evolution of the cosmos, which has so far only partially being completed.

Man

Man – (hereinafter taken to include both men and women) is held to consist of four different 'bodies'. The word body is widely used but does not imply a physical structure but more a collection of energies interpenetrating each other. These bodies are seen as directly relating to the spiritual levels, described above, as follows:

Spirit Body – This is the Divine spark of the one God lying within the heart of every human being. This spark is eternal and enters the individual at birth and leaves at death to continue its journey. The spirit is the bridge between man and the eternal elements of the spiritual world of perfect and complete knowledge, beauty, truth and harmony.

Soul Body - This is the non-permanent part of the incarnated being. It is built during the life and disintegrates with death, but lessons learned during the life are carried forward as part of the spirit body. It is sometimes thought of as having three separate components.

- **The Sentient Soul** – containing sensations, drives, passions and other emotions.
- **The Mind Soul** – containing recollections of practical experience and thoughts.
- **The Consciousness Soul** – seeking universal and objective truths.

Etheric Body – An idea held in the mind of the cosmic creator in the form of a non-material energy model of the physical body, forming and holding the whole in being and keeping individual organs and components running in harmony. With death this body evaporates and allows the physical body to disintegrate.

Physical Body – The flesh and blood body created from indestructible molecules, recognised by conventional science, and held in being by the athletic body. At death this body disintegrates into its components.

Reincarnation

Reincarnation is not recognized by the Christian religion but has always been believed in the East. It is a central tenet of the Wisdom. This is the concept of an individual spark of the Divine repeatedly descending into the material world in order to learn and grow in consciousness and awareness.

This is done in a series lives, in a male or female body, and in a wide variety of roles, as what has to be learned cannot be achieved in one lifetime. The soul returns time and again to learn and grow until reaching the point of complete transformation and oneness with the Divine – and no longer needing to reincarnate.

Karma

Karma is an essential ingredient of the concept of reincarnation. To every action there is a reaction.

'As you sow, so shall you reap.'

In each life, the spirit grows in consciousness and awareness and carries out both positive and negative actions. Positive actions help the spirit to grow towards its ultimate objective. Negative actions have to be compensated for and healed and do so by returning to the initiator, but this time inflicted by another. These karmic reactions return to the individual over and over again, and in life after life, until their lessons are finally learned.

The Purpose of Each Life

Starting as a spark of the divine, the individual spirit is born and reborn in the material world and, through the experiences gained, grows in love, awareness, wisdom and compassion. The objective is to raise the level of consciousness to the point where the soul is reunited with the Divine.

Each life has the intent to:

- heal negative karma from the past,
- create new positive karma and avoid new negative karma,
- learn what is still to be learnt,
- serve, using the talents and skills acquired in past and present lives,
- lead an active, fulfilling and loving life.

Advanced Spirits

Certain advanced spirits have developed to the point where they no longer need to reincarnate but are available as helpful intermediaries between the Divine One and individual incarnate souls. These advanced souls are recognised in many forms including inspirers of individual religions, such as Jesus, Buddha and Mohammed, avatars, saints, masters and guides. They are available as teachers and guides for incarnate individuals and are a part of the ladder of consciousness.

Ebb and Flow

An essential belief of the Wisdom is that the only constant is a state of change following a rhythm of ebb and flow. This movement is seen in the tides of the ocean, the seasons and the breath. It occurs, over longer periods, in human and animal life, in businesses, community projects and in still longer periods in nations and empires. The pattern is birth, growth, a plateau of maturity, and then gentle decay and finally death. An understanding of this 'Breathing of Energy' is helpful when working with the changes experienced in the material world, such as the regular periods of economic growth and recession.

Here we have concentrated upon aspects of the Wisdom affecting our core subject of spiritually inspired community projects. Other features of the Wisdom are listed in the Appendix at the back of this book and these may give ideas for further research.

Practice

The Wisdom defines the objective of the human spirit as growing and developing in awareness and consciousness to the point where 'oneness' with the divine is reached. Most spiritual paths accept this 'oneness' as only being achievable through the use of certain practices.

Around the third century A.D., the Christian Desert Fathers taught attunement with the divine as being reached through fasting, prayer and deprival of bodily comforts. In the sixth century, St. Benedict set up various monasteries and established his famous Rule, giving a broader view of monastic life of:

***Prayer, learning, disciplined living,
and active practical work in the community.***

Benedict's Rule was written for his monks and gives a balanced, rounded and humane view of the way in which the spiritual life should be conducted within the monastery. It is worth reading as much of it is applicable to a spiritual life lived in the world today. Some of the points arising from the Rule, and the teachings of the Wisdom, directly relating to a non-monastic contemporary spiritual life, are as follows. These are given in alphabetical order.

Detachment

A crucial quality is detachment. We would not be alive without our emotions, but we need to be watchful lest they become destructive and obsessive, leading to jealousy, envy, greed, possessiveness and rage. We observe these feelings in a calm, objective fashion without being swept away by them.

We also need to be on our guard against desires subtly presenting themselves as spiritual, but which may be selfish. Below are some typical examples of these phenomena.

To See Results – When a clear objective is established, it is natural to expect positive results. Sometimes the original concept is not met and this may feel like failure. If true inspiration is followed, the emerging, different reality is in fact a stepping-stone towards a long-term concept that had not previously been understood. Detachment is needed in the knowledge that the divine will has been served.

Recognition – Having successfully completed a task, a desire may arise for this wonderful piece of work to be acknowledged and praised. But work carried out anonymously often achieves more positive results than talking about these splendid achievements. Acceptance of lack of acknowledgment is part of treading the path.

Premature Sharing – The desire to be appreciated, as a wise and spiritual being, often leads to the temptation to share thoughts and plans with others too early. Revelations made too soon are often counter-productive. They may result in some initial support, but negative attacks are almost certain to follow, undermining enthusiasm for the project. It is wiser to work silently at the new concept until it develops a real life of its own. Only then should the idea be shared with others.

To Be Liked – This desire can cause all sorts of problems. Certain actions, necessary as part of the divine plan, will involve difficult decisions involving colleagues. Reality needs to be faced and action taken, but, wherever possible, this should be carried out in a compassionate manner. Even though carefully handled, this may result in hurt feelings, but the task must not be shirked through the fear of being disliked.

Disciplined Living

Discipline is the very essence of the spiritual life. In the monastery it involves a rigid and unvarying timetable of prayer, learning and work. This is not appropriate in a contemporary life but some form of rhythm and regular practice is needed.

Learning

Growth in knowledge and understanding of the world of the spirit is a continuing task. There is a danger that we may think we have 'arrived' and no further work is necessary. This is most unlikely and there is always more to learn through reading, courses and working with others.

Prayer

Prayer is the practice of approaching the divine in an attitude of worship and supplication and is the method most often taught and found in exoteric church services. It is equally applicable as a private practice outside the church and, in one form or another, needs to be part of the regular pattern of living.

Material Needs

Benedict understood that the needs of his monks for clothing, accommodation, food, and tools had to be met if they were to be free to carry out their spiritual practice. This reflects the teaching of the Wisdom and is as appropriate today as it was in the days of Benedict.

Living a spiritual life today is complex in that the individual needs to generate income in order to support himself and this may not be generated directly by the task he feels called to do. Fortunately, experience shows that in these cases, all material needs are met. The income needed may not arise directly from the work carried out but will be provided, often in an unforeseen way from an unexpected source.

Meditation

Meditation and contemplation are methods of 'listening' rather than worshipping or 'asking'. These practices are used by the esoteric, mystical branches of established religions and seldom found in the outer exoteric form of these religions. Meditation is now widely used by non-monastic contemporary practitioners of various forms of spirituality and in many different names and guises.

Essentially the practice involves sitting in a quiet place for 20 or 30 minutes, holding the attention centred either on a word, the breath, or some other method of stilling the mind. Direct contact with the divine is made in the stillness of the quiet mind. Thoughts arise, are recognised as distractions and allowed to float away. This is a simple concept but takes application and time to master.

Practical Work

Those on a spiritual path face a conflict between 'being' and 'doing'. This is not a question of either one or the other but a need for both. 'Being' and listening is the start but is only effective when translated into the 'doing' of action for the benefit of all.

The Wisdom defines the concept of the individual honouring the call of the divine through work in the world in form of 'Selfless Service', which is:

'Service with no return save that of serving the Plan.'

Each person reaches his own understanding of his call and area of service. Very often this task will appear to be materially difficult and unrewarding, but once undertaken will bring satisfaction, fulfilment and contentment – difficult to achieve by other means.

Serenity

We are looking at aspects of living in tune with the spirit. In the hectic, intense and busy world in which we live, a calm and tranquil approach is not only helpful but also necessary. The well-known serenity prayer is a useful guide:

God, grant me:
The serenity to accept the things I cannot change,
the courage to change the things I can,
and the wisdom to know the difference.

Worry about things that cannot be changed dissipates effort and emotion and they are best accepted with good grace. That which can be changed needs to be tackled with energy, drive and enthusiasm.

Serenity is the ability to remain calm in the midst of dramatic and frightening events and to remain detached from perceived disastrous results. If we focus on serving the divine, we learn to accept with equanimity all situations as they arise. There is a classic esoteric saying:

'The master is never perturbed.'

We may not become masters and so can expect to sometimes be perturbed, however, perturbation is not a disaster if we face difficulties bravely and firmly and keep steadily moving forward, despite pitfalls and obstructions.

Perhaps, patience should also be added here. A time may come when the objects of the project may appear to have changed or no longer be relevant. Tenacity is required to keep going until clarity emerges.

Truth

The Wisdom says there is one truth described in many ways, but:

'Only that which echoes in your heart, is true for you.'

Reading widely and exploring new ideas is part of the path. But we need to keep our clear understanding of what is true for us. The way that we see truth does not necessarily have to be the same as everyone else's but it has to be true for us.

Will

Development and use of the will is vital on the path and is used to discipline the thoughts and to focus upon the objective. It is useful to explore the different methods of training and perfecting the will.

The Journey

The Wisdom teaches that, for those who wish to follow it, there is a pattern to each individual incarnate life that is a 'Spiritual Journey' or 'Path'. The stages on this journey are as follows:

Conception

We wrote about Karma in the chapter on Wisdom. One of the purposes of each life is to heal negative Karma from the past, to create 'good Karma', and to avoid creating further bad Karma. By these actions all Karma is redeemed and there is no longer a need to reincarnate.

In the period between incarnations the individual spirit becomes aware that a new material life is needed. With the help of the guidance available, the place and situation is chosen with the best conditions to help the growth of the spirit. This will include parents who donate the genes needed to build the body for the next life and provide the environment in which the child will grow in its early days. The situation chosen may superficially appear to be far from ideal but is what is needed for the particular life.

In due course the reincarnating spirit enters the new being.

Birth

The child brings with him the experience of previous incarnations and the needs to be met in order to continue his spiritual growth. He shares DNA with his siblings and may be physically similar to them. But he will often have a different personality, as the previous lives were not the same.

Childhood

The child absorbs the philosophy and teaching of his parents and goes to a school, university or training of their choosing. Whilst this is part of the spirit's plan, the growing child will not be aware that he made this decision, as he will have forgotten his previous lives.

The child develops and matures.

Young Adulthood

The young adult grows in the environment and community of his parents and chooses a career appropriate to this setting. He is usually content with this and does his best to grow and learn contemporary practical skills. He may marry and acquire a sense of responsibility to his family and the community at large.

His intellectual and emotional experiences develop and some wisdom and maturity is acquired.

Awakening Adult

The Wisdom concept of the length of life is 'three score years and ten'. Half way through is the age of 35 and from this time on, Wisdom assumes the individual has attained the experience and skills needed to work in his field of spiritual service, which may be different to his previous work.

This period of awakening often starts with restlessness – a feeling that there must be more to life than so far experienced; the spirit is calling and asking him to awake to 'who he is' and the nature of his true task. To someone steeped in practical materialism, these promptings may appear to be confusing, impractical and unrealistic. This is a critical moment when a choice has to be made – whether to follow the calling of the spirit, or continue on the established track of most of his contemporaries.

Many people respond to this call with the decision to carry on as they are and with the expectations of their fellows. Some answer this 'faint beat of a distant drum' and start an active 'searching' process.

Search

Having made the decision to follow this subtle prompting, there may come a difficult and confusing period. The Wisdom holds guidance as being provided freely and in an unsolicited fashion in the first half of life. Once this basic learning process is complete, further assistance is only provided if specifically requested. The classic expression of this is seen in Mathew Chapter 7.7 of the Christian Bible's New Testament.

> *Ask, and it shall be given you;*
> *seek, and ye shall find;*
> *knock, and it shall be opened unto you.*

The concept of asking for help from a disincarnate being in a numinous world may at first be difficult to accept. Nonetheless if the call is strong, the individual with take the following steps:

- Read books on mysticism and spirituality, attend courses and workshops, consider joining a Mystery School and find a mature adult able to offer help and share their personal experiences.

- Accept the concept of a spiritual world providing help if certain practices are followed.

- Start a spiritual 'practice' and learn how to access divine wisdom.

- Listen to the inspiration received and understand its ability to make a positive contribution to decision making.

- Begin to visualise the future field of service.

Refining Skills

The individual has learned something of the world of the spirit and how to access and use the help available. Now comes the time to remember the latent skills from previous lives and to follow out whatever further training is needed to perfect them. To be useful this ability needs to be relevant to the contemporary situation – talents working well in ancient times may need to be adapted to the present.

If he listens, a subtle prompting will be heard. This may, initially, seem an improbable suggestion and it needs courage to accept this idea as valid. Now comes the time to make another difficult decision – to follow the inspiration of the spirit or to keep going in what most of his family and contemporaries think to be a practical and sensible course of action.

The spiritual path often asks us to leave the security of the material world and start out into an apparently financially risky new venture. This calls for courage, competence and confidence in the validity of the received inspiration. The Wisdom says:

'If you follow your divine call, your needs will be met.'

The new task does not itself need to be income generating. The necessary resources will always be provided even though from a separate and often unexpected source. Faith that this will be so is what makes this difficult decision possible.

Service

If the available guidance is followed, a time will come when the new field of service becomes apparent.

This will be the area in which the latent skills, learnt over many lives, coupled with the experience gained in the present life are combined to the point where the individual is able to be a useful and fluent instrument of the divine.

This is not achieved in a single step. Inspiration continues throughout life, as will a steady increase in learning, experience and spiritual usefulness.

Vigilance

Awareness is needed on every stage of this journey.

We may be satisfied with a conventional career and go on to great things in the material world whilst denying the call of the spirit.

If we respond to the call of the spirit, we may become so entranced with the psychic wonders occurring in our life that we think everything possible has been achieved whilst not realising that these phenomena are part of the journey and not an end in themselves.

Or we may get stuck in our field of service, assuming that we have achieved all that is necessary, whilst ignoring subtle promptings to move into something new and to use our ever improving skills in a fresh and more productive manner.

Outcome

If the spiritual call is understood and followed then comes:

*** The peace of mind that passes all understanding.***

Working with the divine is not always simple, but, if followed with commitment, it brings joy, fulfilment and quiet contentment.

Guidance

The wisdom says:

Through prayer and invocation individuals are able to access and communicate with the wisdom of advanced spirits on the higher levels of the spiritual plane.

Let us look at how we set about using this guidance.

A spark of the Divine is within each individual – this is the eternal Spirit, the vehicle by which the individual is able to access the divine. By raising his level of consciousness, the individual is able to access ever-higher levels of the Wisdom. The spiritual world contains a range of entities, with levels of consciousness extending from the most mundane to the most spiritual, many of who are committed to helping the individuals on their journey. Thus a person, at any level of development, is able to find a spiritual entity with whom he can be in harmony, and whose guidance he will understand. How does he do this?

An esoteric saying is:

'When the pupil is ready, the Master appears.'

The concept is that the guide will find the one to be guided, if and when he is ready to receive this guidance. When the time is right, the master will make contact in any one of a number of different ways. It may be through a Mystery School, a book, a lecture, wise words from a friend, or intuitive ideas whilst meditating. Whatever the method, the appropriate spiritual entity will make contact.

Guidance may change as the individual grows in consciousness. A stage may be completed, and a different teacher may be appropriate. Throughout this process, the need to be open-minded, to listen, and use discrimination, continues to be necessary.

Who are these guides and what is their purpose?

Purpose

This guidance is twofold: to help the individual to grow spiritually, and to provide an understanding of the part to be played in the divine plan. The guide, a benign being, has the interests of the growth in awareness and consciousness of the whole human race, and the instruction of the individual will always be within the context of the broader interests of humanity as a whole.

The concept of divine entities guiding humankind to an ever more loving and fruitful world, can sometimes be difficult to accept. We appear to be living today in a world growing in selfishness and ruthlessness rather than compassion and love. Nonetheless, the Wisdom holds all is for the best. If this indeed be so, then maybe we are going through a time of trial, which will lead to an ever-clearer understanding of the inevitable negative results of a materialistic society. From this may come realisation of the fundamental changes needed if society is to move towards a more loving and compassionate world.

What form will be taken by these helpful guides?

Discarnate Guides

Guidance is always available at a level, and in a form, appropriate to the state of consciousness achieved by the individual. Discarnate guides are found in a wide variety of apparent guises, including Tibetan Masters, Chinese emperors, Native American Indians, Goddesses, Shamanic teachers, and priests of every sort.

These guides exist in a non-material spiritual form incomprehensible to an incarnate being. They therefore appear in a guise recognizable to the one they are seeking to guide. It is held that it takes considerable effort to generate such a shape.

Living Guides

A guru is a living personality who is held to be of great wisdom and sanctity and able to provide positive guidance to the devotee. The guidance comes whilst in the presence of the guru, but is not always in the form of spoken words. In recent years, Eastern gurus such as Sai Baba, the Maharishi and Mother Meera have gained a significant following in the West.

Accessing Guidance

Once the appropriate guidance has been contacted, the next step is to learn how to communicate.

This is achieved by developing the intuition: the subtle part of the mind able to contact the universal consciousness. This 'Still Inner Voice' delivers concepts and ideas, often without prior intellectual thought. Awareness, understanding and acceptance of the intuition are available to all, but we need to develop and enhance these faculties if the intuition is to become a useful and powerful tool.

Our present paradigm tends not to value intuition, often looked upon as 'merely imagination'. This is surprising as every scientific discovery, invention and creative work, started with a flash of intuition. Whilst the intellect may be used to develop the initial spark, the intuition remains behind the original idea.

Poets and writers speak of their 'Muse' inspiring them. The Greeks had a variety of specific muses, each specialising in a particular type of poetry, writing or music. Contemporary musicians speak of the work 'pouring through them' from some unknown source.

We need to be able to accept our intuition as the means through which we receive the voice of the entity seeking to guide us. Inspired ideas may reach us through our minds, but may also be triggered off by situations or the words of others; all of which are possible vehicles for the message. The unusual nature of this communication requires a different approach to 'listening'.

There are a number of ways in which we can develop and enhance our intuition and our ability to contact the divine.

Meditation and Prayer

Mentioned in the chapter on 'Practice'.

Being in Nature

One of the most effective methods of accessing the divine is walking, or sitting in nature and opening the soul to attunement with the world of the spirit. This should be in some beautiful place – sitting by the sea and watching the gentle breaking of the waves; on a hill with distant vistas of rolling countryside, or in a forest, observing the dappled sunlight, and listening to the movement of a multitude of living creatures in the undergrowth.

Practical Means

This is the process of accessing the divine by using some form of device. A number of tools are available, including quasi-scientific instruments, such as Radionics and other instruments of this type. Most recognised is the practice of dowsing – a rod or pendulum is used to enhance the sensitivity of the individual's reception. This is a productive way of using a device to enhance the intuitive faculties.

Divination

These are methods used for help in accessing the divine. They include the 'I-Ching': a forecasting method of casting coins or yarrow sticks in a sequence of six, noting results and interpreting these by using the 'Divining Book of the I-Ching'.

Tarot cards belong to this category. The tarot reader deals out and read cards in the presence of the client. Interpretation of the fall of the cards, combined with the sensitivity and intuition of the reader, can lead to a perceptive and useful result.

Included, is the whole world of astrology. This is a field of knowledge, supported and attested by thousands of years of research and findings. In the hands of an experienced and skilled astrologer a reading can produce perceptive and helpful insights.

Channelling

Channelling is a method of hearing and recording the voice of what appears to be a third person. This is recognised in books such as 'Seth Speaks'. It is also a useful tool when used to access personal guidance. This requires the acceptance of valid guidance being available, and the ability to 'hear' and record what comes through.

'Hearing' guidance is an interesting process in itself. This is not received as an aurally recorded sound coming through the ether. Rather, awareness in the mind of words being spoken. The ability to accept the validity of these words as coming from a third party is the essence of channelling. The process is to sit in a quiet place, ask a specific question, and wait for the answer to start flowing.

A number of practical methods are used including:

Automatic Writing – as with all methods of accessing the intuition, practice is needed. What seems to work best is to write the first word that comes into the mind, and then to continue with the flow that comes through. There may be a tendency to dismiss this as a figment of the imagination, but faith is needed in the reality of the guidance being received.

The secret is to keep the practical, logical, everyday mind out of the way during the session.

Verbal Channelling – For many people, this is a simpler and more effective way of working than automatic writing. In this case, a decision is made on how best to record the message. This could be with a voice recorder, later transcribed in writing. Now, with the availability of voice-recognition software, the simplest way is to dictate the whole session straight into a computer for printing later.

Intuitive Sparks

Once the intuition is developed as a way of accessing guidance, the individual will begin to recognise the sparks and ideas, received throughout the day. Ideas flash into the consciousness and disappear again. Even without setting up any formal apparatus for accessing these thoughts, they, nonetheless, arrive of their own volition. These ideas are often valuable and should be kept in mind or recorded. It is worth carrying a small notebook in which to note these sparks of intuition.

Synchronicity

A synchronous experience is a fortuitous but meaningful occurrence, i.e. meeting the person you want to see, feeling drawn to enter a particular bookshop and finding the perfect book waiting on a shelf. This is a way for the intuition to pass on information. Accepting synchronous events as having a meaning encourages further similar communication.

To help this process flow we need to accept that there are no accidents. Every event is significant, although it is not always easy to understand the meaning.

Dreams

For millennia the interpretation of dreams was accepted as useful. This appreciation gradually disappeared, but depth psychologists have increased our awareness of the value of understanding dreams and a wide selection of books is available on the subject. Dreams are a way of accessing the unconscious and could be said to be closer to the intuition and the spiritual world than the conscious, awakened mind.

Only the individual dreamer is able to understand the real meaning of his dreams, but experienced professionals can help with the interpretation. An excellent practice is to make a point of recording dreams and endeavouring to interpret them. Recalling the dream in a notebook on waking is best, as dreams tend to disappear rapidly after waking up.

Keeping a Journal

An essential part of the process of hearing and accessing spiritual messages is to keep a journal. A loose-leaf notebook is best as handwritten thoughts, automatic writing notes, transcribed notes of every sort, and other significant experiences can all be included.

One of the intriguing things about a spiritual journal is how the words – when first recorded – often appear to be banal and obvious. Upon reading the journal again, in a week or so, it is then found that these notes have given an accurate forecast of how things would develop and contained words of extraordinary wisdom. We should not be surprised if these words appear to be wise, inspiring and constructive, as the whole object of the exercise of the journal has been to access the divine world of infinite beauty and truth.

Like everything on the spiritual journey, learning how to access guidance is an individual business. Each person has to explore and find the ways that work best for him.

Spiritual Projects

Glastonbury

We are exploring how to set up and run spirit-inspired projects in an environment with a strong sacred energy and a suitable community. My experience is in Glastonbury, UK, where such conditions exist. Whilst this town is not unique, a study of a specific example will be helpful.

History

Glastonbury, in Bronze Age times was held to be a holy place; a prominent conical hill, on a remote island surrounded by tidal marshes with only a narrow causeway leading to higher ground in the east. In the early first century, we find traces of resident hermits and a legend of a visit by Joseph of Arimathea and his young nephew, Jesus.

Why did these early inhabitants identify this as a sanctuary? The answer is the 'Numinous Energy' in the landscape.

The place attracted mystics whose prayers reinforced the existing atmosphere. The original hermitage grew into an established monastery coming into historical focus in the 10th century with the thriving Benedictine Abbey, its Abbott Dunstan, and pilgrim visitors drawn from afar.

To support the monks and visitors, a small town grew up around the abbey, supplying the services of candle makers, launderers, butchers, bakers and assorted others. So we see a spiritual heart supported by a secular town. Economic harmony reigned as wealth brought to the monastery by pilgrims and patrons flowed out to support the town. The abbey was a dominant landlord, owning most of the houses, farms and manors for miles around, and many local people were tenants. The dependence of the town upon the monks for economic prosperity was accepted, but there could be resentment, when they were seen to be over-authoritative.

With the dissolution of the monasteries and the destruction of the abbey, the spiritual heart, and most of the income of Glastonbury was lost. For many years, various efforts were made to find an alternative source of revenue, but with little success, and the town drifted into becoming a small, isolated market centre.

In the 19th century, a renewal of activity occurred with the arrival of the railway and canal. The improved access to the rest of the country opened new markets and potential for increased sale of local products. The Morland and the Clark families built factories to process sheepskin and make shoes, providing jobs for the blue-collar workers, and, for a time, the economy was buoyant.

After the Second War, the cost of manufacturing footwear locally became too high and production was moved overseas with only a distribution centre remaining. There also came a decline in the demand for sheepskin products. As a result most of the local factories were closed, with the loss of some 1,500 jobs – a major blow to such a small community.

With the closure of the abbey, few pilgrims arrived, but people interested in local history continued to visit. The post-war years saw a slow revival of interest in Glastonbury as a pilgrimage town. This started with hippy travellers, and a reputation as a worldwide sacred site began to grow. Since then, visits by a new type of tourist – pilgrims in a modern guise – have increased and today are some forty per cent of all visitors. Many stay for a number of days in B&Bs and hotels, spend money in shops and cafes, attend workshops and courses and become customers of therapists. This is in contrast to the majority of conventional tourists, who tend to make day visits.

Landscape

Glastonbury is held by some to be a 'thin place' where the spiritual world is closer than the norm. In early times this could be experienced in the hills, the streams, the woods and the marshes full of fish and fowl; a place burgeoning with earthly and spiritual life.

Today, much is changed but the atmosphere remains. Meadows and woodland still exist and an awareness of the closeness and reality of nature can be felt when walking in the sacred sites of Chalice Well, Bride's Mound and the grounds of the ruined abbey. In the countryside, around the Tor, lies what is claimed to be the Glastonbury Zodiac: a pattern of natural features, which appear to reflect on earth the pattern passing of the constellations in the sky.

Somehow, this sacred numinous environment has survived the recent large-scale building of houses, supermarkets and modern infrastructure.

'Over-lighting Energy'

In the chapter on guidance, we discussed the spiritual help available to humans. In Glastonbury this appears as an 'Over-Lighting Energy', which seeks to assist the town achieve its true destiny. It is available in a shape recognizable to the individual seeking help and takes many forms, including the 'Angel of Glastonbury', 'the Goddess' and a group of long-dead monks: the 'Company of Avalon'.

This guiding principal has an understanding of the ultimate objective for Glastonbury. It knows what is needed in the way of resources and sets about making these available. If it is focussed upon and asked for help, it will make a contribution to the positive results of the activities of the individual.

Purpose

If the over-lighting energy has a purpose for the town, what might this be?

The 'Purpose of Glastonbury' is not widely discussed and this is understandable in the present paradigm where the creation of material projects is understood but the concept of a spiritual motivation is not.

The Wisdom teaches that spiritual purpose is the essence of the meaning of life. In this context, it might be said that the purpose of the town is to:

- become a spiritual centre of love, learning and personal transformation;

- attract the people and resources needed to achieve this end;

- help visitors and residents to grow in consciousness and develop their skills, in the service of the community.

A 'Glastonbury Experience'

A personal pattern experienced by some of those 'called' to the town is often called a 'Glastonbury Experience', whose stages are as follows:

The Awakening – The individual has achieved a degree of fluency in the material world and awareness of the spiritual.

The Call – The over-lighting energy of Glastonbury knows a particular talent is needed. A telepathic message is put out to attract a person who is receptive and able to meet this need. This is couched in terms that are attractive but may not reveal the ultimate purpose.

An individual will respond. This intuitive prompting may at first seem irrational, but gradually the necessity to answer this call will overcome the doubts. The recipient is entirely free to accept or reject the call, but if he decides to accept, he will make his way to Glastonbury.

Arriving – The town appears familiar to the newcomer and, possibly for the first time, he is surrounded by people to whom he can talk freely about his spiritual life. He is excited with the potential and sets out to make friends and establish himself.

Testing – He may then experience the strong reaction known as the 'Glastonbury Experience'. This takes the form of a 'dark night of the soul' where he is brought face to face with his own frailty and shadow. Things seem to fall apart and difficulties arise in relationships, work, and accommodation. His strength and purpose is being tested by the over-lighting energy.

Decision – he now has to decide if he has the temperament to work happily in this unusual atmosphere, or whether he would be more comfortable elsewhere. This is a personal decision and carries no value judgment.

'Settling in' – If he decides to stay in the town, then comes a period of discovering the work he is asked to do.

He may have thought he was leaving his conventional life to serve in a new and spiritually orientated manner, but Glastonbury needs not only his latent talents, but also his practical experience of the material world. He may be disturbed and find that his experience as a spiritual counsellor is not needed, but rather his skills as an accountant.

In one form or another, the task involves 'selfless service'. This may not be directly financially rewarded, but there will be the huge benefit of an acceleration of personal growth and the satisfaction of making a contribution towards the fulfilment of the purpose of the town.

Glastonbury Today

The original town grew as a supplier of services to the abbey. With the dissolution of the monastery it lost its spiritual centre; but Glastonbury is a place of transformation and, to achieve its true potential, it must return to the balance of a mystic heart with a supporting town.

The Alternative Community - The Mystic heart is beginning to emerge in a contemporary guise. Of the resident population of some 10,000, about one third would say they were 'called' to Glastonbury and experience some sort of a spiritual purpose. They are supplying the specialized services needed to support the spiritual aspects of the place, and are known locally as the alternative community – a brief summary of who they are, is as follows:

- They are men and women of various ages who have achieved a sustainable way of living.

- They are not living together in one commune but are scattered about in their own dwellings, all over Glastonbury.

- They have a wide range of religious and spiritual beliefs, some of which are unconventional, as is often their appearance!

- They provide, manage and staff most of the centres, sacred sites, shops, therapies, courses and workshops serving the needs of visiting pilgrims.

- Their number includes a range of artistic and creative skills, including musicians, artists, writers and computer experts.

In 1985, the alternative community was small and rather like a specialised college in one corner of the town. Most of the members knew each other and were involved in a number of local projects. The long-term residents recognized these newcomers, but tended not to be in sympathy with their activities.

Today, this group has grown in number and has come to resemble a 'University' with 'Faculties' – groups of people running individual projects but not necessarily knowing or being involved with others. There are the beginnings of an understanding by the town that these unusual services are attracting more visitors and contributing to the economy as a whole.

The passing years have seen a marked change in the interests of the alternative community and visitors to the town. In the 1980s, many were focussed upon the 'Esoteric Energies' and in products so related. Today, there is broader range of interests and shopkeepers note a significant change in buying patterns.

The Internet also has had an effect. Following a spiritual path used to involve substantial research in discovering the right books, courses and teachers. Today, the web instantly reveals a wide range of teaching. In some ways this short-circuits the sense of 'seeking and finding' and may lead to a premature belief in having 'arrived'. Also, the Wisdom maintains the early stages of the path should be conducted within a specific spiritual tradition – this easy access to information may develop a more general and superficial approach.

People continue to be called and the alternative community steadily grows. The new members are not as socially unconventional as in the past and this reflects the changes taking place in society at large. There is a growing awareness of climate change, green and collective issues, and a sense that pure materialism and economic growth is not working. With this has gone a declining interest in the specifically spiritual. The alternative community and the town are growing more alike.

This community has a growing awareness of itself, although it is still fragmented. There are groups and centres where occasional events take place with the participation of the whole community, but there is a lack of overall cooperation and cohesion. Each group and individual will need to understand their role with complete clarity if the town, as a whole, is to move forward.

The 'Secular' Town - What we are calling the secular town does not fully understand the town's emerging new role. We are not using the term 'secular' in a pejorative sense, but simply to define its difference from what we are calling the spiritual heart. This 'secular town' is delivering all the services as in the days of the abbey, and is just as essential to the life of the town today. Hence, it is vital that we understand the different aspects and roles, if the town is to flourish and reach its full potential.

Summary

Today, Glastonbury has an atmosphere that allows people to enhance their own level of consciousness and awareness. This is welcomed by many of the alternative community, but some local residents are disturbed by the growing unconventional nature of their town. Originally, it seemed as if this lack of understanding was an obstruction to progress, but it has become clear that these differences have created a need for clarity of purpose and outreach to others, which has in turn led to a much stronger awareness of the inter-dependence of all parts of the town. The need to reach an understanding with those who see things differently has led to a tempering and moderating of extreme points of view, and a redefining of some aspects of how the truth is seen. Building these bridges is leading towards a closer understanding than would otherwise have been achieved. This growing awareness of the value of all people and services will, hopefully, eventually lead to a balanced understanding that will be more wholesome than was the case in the time of the monks.

We have had a brief look at one individual place with a strong spiritual and esoteric history; how for many years it lost some of its spiritual energy and how it is now rediscovering its true purpose. Experience gained in this town is the basis for this book, but similar conditions and experiences will be found in other places with a strong spiritual background.

More information about Glastonbury is given in Appendix 2 at the back of this book.

Balance

We are looking at how we create successful spiritually inspired community projects. Spirituality is the inspiration behind all such ventures, but they need to be created within the facilities and practices of the present materialistic paradigm. The key to success is to hold a balance between these conflicting scenarios and the next stage in our journey is to look at this paradox.

Materialism

Over the last 200 years, the development of the sciences, and their remarkable achievements, has created an emphasis on materialism. The basis of this is the empirical method, whereby a new theory is produced by an individual scientist, tested by others and, if the same result is achieved, accepted as a valid finding. It will be taken as a law if further experiments consistently show the same result. This approach has resulted in a wealth of new discoveries including those in communication, travel and allopathic medicine.

With the invention of the steam engine came the ability to harness power. With the understanding of electricity came the ability to transmit this power for use at a distance from its source. For the first time in the history of humankind, abundant power could be supplied anywhere, whereas before the only sources were localised water, wind and animal or human labour. This new source of power enabled factories to be established resulting in the mass migration from the countryside to the towns.

These two new avenues of development, science and accessible energy, generated a rising standard of living, with its labour saving device. With the rapid increase in scientific knowledge came a substantial improvement in health. People live longer and cures are available for a host of previously fatal diseases. This phenomenon is most marked in the West, but the rest of the world is catching up.

Material progress has a negative side. Starting with Newton and Descartes, nature came to be seen as a mechanical device, understandable by the application of mechanics and mathematics. This approach left little room for the divine or any form of spiritual influence.

All natural resources – the trees, creatures in the sea, beasts in the field, minerals – are seen as being freely available for harvest by humans to meet their material needs. The result is a finite supply of ores hungrily excavated from the earth and turned into physical products, often of an ephemeral nature. After a short life, these artefacts end up in landfill sites generating methane gas. This destructive action transforms limited useful resources into useless and dangerous rubbish.

This process is going on at an accelerating rate with almost complete disregard for its impact on the health of the planet. The pollution of the atmosphere and seas, caused by dirty methods of generating power, is leading to a man-made contribution to climate change, global warming, disturbance of weather patterns, and the destruction of animal species. The concept of our world having a powerful and sensitive spiritual presence has been lost.

This situation has arisen with the growing dominance of a simplistic scientific outlook. Successes are achieved through the use of empirical and practical methods, based upon the ability to measure the movements and effects of material objects.

> **'If it cannot be seen, felt, heard or measured,
> then it does not exist.'**

The Newtonian concept of nature being comparable to a machine, with separate individual components meshing with each other, led to the idea that pieces of the mechanism could be studied individually without taking into account their relationship to the whole. Previously the study of Natural Philosophy embraced all aspects of the organic and inorganic cosmos. Now narrow specialisation has arisen; producing an abundance of knowledge, but with the loss of the idea of the universe as integrated, complete and alive.

Contemporary science does not include the realm of the mind as a valid subject for research and, in consequence, no concept of a 'Universal Intelligence', embracing and guiding the cosmos, is acceptable. Examining the physical brain and its various electrical functions is allowed, as this is measurable by suitable apparatus, but how ideas form is not a matter that can be investigated scientifically. The assumption is made that thoughts originate solely within the brain and not from an external source.

The world of the spirit may only be realised through subjective personal experience and is not measurable by objective observation. If this inner life cannot be recorded scientifically, then from a material point of view it does not exist and there can be no acceptable concept of an intelligent, compassionate and wise universal consciousness. In consequence, there is no understanding of the ability of the individual to raise his level of spiritual awareness. The only purpose in life must be to concentrate upon physical comfort, the acquisition of factual knowledge and worldly goods – and having fun.

Spirituality

We earlier looked at the world of the spirit. Despite the prevailing materialistic view, some progress is being made in accepting the possibility of a non-physical component to reality. The 'depth psychologists', including Jung, Assagioli, and Maslow, all recognise a 'lower' unconscious and a 'higher' super-conscious. Awareness is growing of a form of intelligence and unity pervading the whole cosmos. In astronomy, discoveries are made almost daily, and it becomes ever more difficult to accept the chance creation of the astonishing array of gas clouds, galaxies, pulsars and red giants.

This new understanding is appearing in publications such as 'The Scientific and Medical Network,' 'Resurgence', and 'Meditation Monthly', and in a range of books endeavouring to explore the ways science and spirituality are compatible. Still only a minority of scientists share this awakening, and the overriding paradigm is one of materialism and denial of the spiritual.

Achieving balance is the essence of the spiritual life. We are confronted on all sides with passionately held views, often diametrically opposed. This dichotomy or paradox occurs everywhere be it socialists versus conservatives, fracking enthusiasts versus anti-frackers, global warming enthusiasts or global warming deniers. The list is endless. Individuals believe their views are correct and those who disagree are not only wrong but may be a danger to society.

The spiritually aware need to remain firmly centred and to listen with an open mind to all views. A more balanced understanding can only be reached when all views have been heard.

The task is to remain firmly centred and to listen with an open mind to all views.

Harmony

Can these two differing outlooks be reconciled? There are encouraging signs that this may be so.

Scientists have difficulty in accepting the concept of spirituality and many spiritually aware people are alarmed at the negative side of pure materialism. The root cause of the schism is the idea that physical proof is needed for a theory to be valid. This requires an external objective view to be the starting point from which measurements and further experiments can be made. In contrast, all spiritual experience is personal and subjective and not measurable in scientific terms and hence often dismissed as nebulous, mysticism and superstition.

This conflict between materialism and spirituality leads to endless misunderstandings, and may well be one of the strongest influences inhibiting the realisation of peace and harmony throughout the world. At present, many are struggling to increase their material standard of living, often with disregard for the impact they are having on the world's ecology. Others are endeavouring to promote their own particular view of religion, sometimes by violent means, with no concern for the effect on non-believers.

Superficially, these seem to be two different approaches. In fact they are not alternatives, but both are essential for harmonious living. Science without spiritual understanding tends to misuse of the earth's resources, threatening our very existence. Spirituality lacking practicality leads to ineffectual projects. Only by accepting the validity and necessity of both these paths, can we reach a wholesome balance. Sadly, this is not what we see today, where the rational-scientific view is dominating, whilst the intuitive, spiritual approach is seen by many as an illusion.

Despite the apparent differences between these two schools of thought, encouraging signs are appearing of a 'reaching out'. Academia is exploring contemporary spirituality and business is embracing the concept of mindfulness. Real progress is being made even though not always apparent.

There is a slow but growing awareness of the validity of both these poles. With spiritually inspiring community projects we cannot afford to wait for full harmony to be achieved, but must work with our own concept of balance.

Glastonbury, as a pilgrimage town, needs 'alternative' people committed to serving the spiritual 'energies' of the place. Projects established will be in harmony with guidance and inspiration but also need to be managed and run in a practical manner. Essential to the efficient running of the town are the services of doctors, lawyers, street cleaners, food shops, cafes and accommodation. Ideally, for success of the whole, the providers of these facilities will understand the work of the spiritual centres.

Both aspects, working in harmony, are necessary if the town is to reach its full potential.

Awareness of the Whole and the need to work with materialism and spirituality is the essence of the projects at which we are looking. This is easily said but not as readily achieved. How we set about this we will discuss next.

Conception

The very start of a community project is an idea.

Before we explore this in more detail we will look at what might be called the 'Creative Process'. This procedure is universal and is found in the creation of everything, whether it be writing a book, creating a piece of music, starting a new political policy or building an ocean liner – the following steps are taken:

- An idea is conceived of the ultimate objective.

- This is visualised in detail and decisions made upon the measures needed to materialise the idea.

- Action is taken to start the creation process.

- The project is continued, through all adversity, until the desired outcome is achieved.

In spiritually inspired community projects there a number of principles lying behind the ideas with which we are working. These are:

'Not-for-profit' – These ventures are often non-profit-making. By this, we mean not paying profits to individuals. If successful, they will generate a surplus to be used only for community purposes.

Abundance – The Wisdom states that, if a project is truly inspired, everything required will be made available at the correct time. This abundant flow meets all needs, whether those of individuals or the project. The understanding and acceptance of this concept is held even when the operation is grappling with a shortage of finance and other resources.

If genuinely inspired, what is required will arrive, not out of thin air, but through some action in the material world.

Selfless service – The idea of personal service to a divinely inspired idea lies at the heart of projects of this nature. This concept implies serving the divine plan even if the allocated task is not immediately appealing. The call is:

'Service without any return save that of serving the Plan.'

Once the nature of the work is clear, no argument should dissuade the individual from fulfilling his assignment. Others may comment and make negative remarks about how they perceive the value of what is being done, but the serving individual is happy to continue regardless.

Practical Skills – Side-by-side with the spiritual emphasis must go a practical approach to the everyday task of running a successful enterprise. Again, these latter skills are similar to those required by a conventional business, albeit with subtle differences.

Balance – We have spoken about balance and the need to embrace both spiritual inspiration and material activity. This approach is essential when creating the projects in which we are interested and is not easy, as the two poles of this dichotomy often seem to be in conflict.

Now let us look at the subject of this chapter – the conception of the original idea.

For a conventional project, an individual 'receives a thought' and understands its purpose. The source of the idea may appear to be personal and the motives will be varied: to make money, to create a beautiful object, to achieve fame, to become successful in politics. The motives are as numerous as individuals but for success there must be a strong sense of purpose.

Here we come across the first and perhaps the most fundamental difference between the projects we are looking at, and more conventional businesses. Our ventures differ in being divinely inspired and supported by guidance throughout their life.

Some of these differences are:

Inspiration

The start of the project is an inspiring idea. We have mentioned the 'over-lighting energy', in Glastonbury having a long-term purpose for the town, and an awareness of the resources needed to bring this into being. These requirements are crystallized into a model on the 'Etheric Plane'. This is a duplicate, complete in every detail, but does not yet exist in physical form. The task now is to materially realise this concept.

Initiation

The over-lighting energy starts the process by projecting a telepathic image of the etheric model. One or more, individuals receive this communication as an idea arising in their mind. These people are on a spiritual path and their minds are open to receiving this type of message.

Several individuals may begin to think about the idea, but usually, only one person feels sufficiently inspired to start taking the first practical steps. Others may have received the same inspiration and will help when the time is appropriate.

This might be thought of as an unusual way of starting a community project. The more usually accepted method is to gather a group of possibly interested people and, with them, explore various ideas. This often involves putting up post-it notes on a pin-board. Based on the main points emerging, the conveners endeavour to put together a plan for the future. Whilst this concept is splendidly democratic, it seldom produces concrete action.

We will call our inspired individual the 'initiator'. He attunes to the messages he is receiving from his aspect of the over-lighting energy. This may take some time, but in due course, a plan begins to emerge and is envisioned in as much detail as is possible at this early stage. Part of this process will be to define the long-term aim and the stages required to reach the objective.

A single individual can achieve little on his own and the initiator has the task of finding suitable helpers. He starts by holding the vision with absolute clarity in his own mind. This sounds what might be called a 'clear note', which enables others to telepathically sense and react to it.

The vision, although held clearly, is still quite fragile and may be something which seems absurd and totally unattainable to the majority of people; hence, the importance of keeping the idea confidential in the early days. Spreading the word too soon may lead to destructive attacks from many quarters, thereby weakening the sense of purpose of the initiator.

From those responding to this initial call will be set up a 'core group' to take the idea forward. This group will be the central creative body steering the project. Its ability to work as an effective and inspired team is the key to long-term success. The initiator holding a clear vision helps all those potentially interested to understand exactly what is intended so that only people who resonate with the plan will want to find out more. This early 'sieving' saves wasting time in talking to those who are not prepared to make the necessary commitment.

As people come forward, the initiator talks to them, bearing in mind the qualities needed. Only if a person has the necessary temperament will he be accepted as part of the core group. The requirements are as follows:

Core Group Qualities

If the group is to flourish, members need to understand and accept the following qualities that will be required by each of them.

Peer Group – Accept that members have different skills, but are of equal worth and able to lead where their experience is appropriate and follow when another member leads. This 'dance of responsibilities' is the essence of a successful core group. For this balance to work, all members need similar 'powers of authority' to enable their individual voices to be heard.

Inspiration – Be inspired by the initiator's vision, aware of the source of this inspiration, and committed to taking the idea to completion.

Awareness – Be on a personal spiritual path and attuned to where this is leading. To understand the need for discipline in keeping in harmony with the original inspiration of the project, be conversant with the 'rules of creativity' and know how to bring the project into materialisation.

Responsibilities – Care passionately about the project, and be prepared to offer the time and work required to bring it to completion. Know that they are stewards, carrying responsibility for the project. If and when they want to retire from the project, they will help find a suitable person to replace them.

Service – Work as voluntary members of the group, but be paid for specific executive tasks, such as treasurer, company secretary or manager. Whatever the remuneration, the role will require time and commitment – often substantially more than anyone expected! As with any spiritual enterprise, the work may be anonymous and unrecognised, but rewarded by the knowledge of having honoured the call to serve a spiritually orientated community project.

Vision – Share the vision. In the early days, this may only be an outline of the ultimate objectives, but as more research is carried out the details will be clarified. From the beginning the planned outcome should be recorded in writing, and modified as things develop. The detailed plan will be for members of the group with summary to help volunteers and staff to understand the purpose and progress being made.

Consensus – Agree a method of making decisions – usually best done by sharing and consensus. Confidentiality is essential whilst a problem is being discussed. Each member will honour agreements reached, regardless of possible reservations.

Flexibility – Be open to suggestions from people outside the group and be prepared to adapt where necessary.

Acceptance – Accept and honour the beliefs held by other members of the group.

Courage – Be prepared to accept responsibility for group decisions. Inevitably, problems arise and it will be necessary to have the confidence to take the correct action even though this may touch upon sensitive personal matters.

Tenacity – Keep going through all adversity in order to give the activity every opportunity to succeed.

Delegation – Be able to delegate. This is a special skill, requiring the ability to choose suitable people and trust in their ability and willingness to carry out the work. This will require keeping a quiet watch to ensure that all is being done correctly. The task is to encourage the individuals to take responsibility and pride in carrying out their duties in an effective manner.

Individual Qualities

In addition to the qualities required by all members of the group, certain individual qualities, skills and talents are also needed. Missing skills will have to be found from volunteers, paid staff, consultants or professional advisers. Each member of the group should be quite clear about his own contribution, and those made by the other members.

These qualities are as follows:

Vision Holders – All members have accepted the project as being spiritually inspired. Now one or more people need to continue the connection with the initiating guidance. This task is not as simple as might first appear. A stream of ideas will be pouring in from volunteers, members of the staff and the community at large, whilst at the same time there is always the temptation to remain too firmly fixed on the original concept. The vision holders need to continue in attunement with the guidance available, using discernment and discrimination in deciding what changes are appropriate.

From time to time the vision will be updated, redefined, rewritten, and circulated amongst all those involved in the project, so that they may understand the way things are developing.

Entrepreneurial Spirit – Creating a new project needs not only divine inspiration but also an entrepreneurial spirit. How do we define such an attitude? The word 'entrepreneur' conjures up visions of people dedicated to making money. The reality is rather different, as the true innovator is motivated by a passion to create the product. Wealth is a possible by-product of successfully realising the idea.

Additional qualities required are: imagination, a clear objective, enthusiasm, tenacity, courage, tireless dedication, consistency of purpose, and the ability to take risks. The government and academic world pay lip service to the need for entrepreneurs but have little understanding of the fearless and buccaneering spirit of these individuals.

Some of these qualities are required when creating a spiritual activity. The initiator needs to ensure that the core group contains adventurous spirits to provide the courage and energy needed to help the project to flourish, particularly when opposition is experienced.

Management – Experience of managing practical businesses, charities and not-for-profit organisations.

Maintainers – This is a special skill that does not have the excitement of starting a new venture but is the capacity to maintain the momentum of something already started. In some ways, this is a repetitive job, but one with its own satisfaction and fulfilment. Personal contact with the volunteers and staff is involved plus the expertise to sort out emotional dramas in a calm fashion. Also required is the ability to monitor progress and make changes where necessary. For the right person, this is a rewarding task.

Decision Makers – Some or all of the group members will have to reach conclusions and make decisions. These will often be difficult, involving an element of risk affecting people and funds. These individuals need to be reliable and confident, able to decide what has to be done and to carry out the necessary actions, regardless of consequences. People with this responsibility, who care too much about being loved, will always be inhibited in their actions. They must be prepared to be disliked!

'Ameliorators' – There will be disagreements and emotional upsets, hence a need for members able to deal with these situations, and who are suitably empowered to make fair decisions respecting the concerns of those involved whilst caring about the interests of the project as a whole.

We are looking at a rather strange creature – a peer group of equals, with differing skills, guided by intuition and without a rigid hierarchical structure. This very flexibility brings with it a responsibility for clarity. Roles and tasks need to be allocated to enable all members to know who does what, and how decisions are made. Usually, the member responsible for a particular activity recommends the action to be taken and the group as a whole make the final decision.

The core group carries responsibility for planning the enterprise and making key decisions. They need to ensure that amongst their members, recruited volunteers, staff and professional advisers, are people with the skills to carry

Creating Spirituality Inspired Projects – Conception

out, or supervise, all the duties required in running any project. This will usually include a chairperson, a manager, a treasurer, a company secretary, plus people experienced in delivering the services being established. These specific tasks are applicable to any business and we need not amplify them here.

So, the original conception process is complete. A small group share the vision and are committed to its materialisation.

The task is now to start bringing the idea into physical reality.

Birth

Once the core group has been established, the next stage is to decide how the project is to be run and the resources required. The needs here will be similar to those of a conventional business but with subtle differences including the following:

Business plan

The group may not be running a business but they still need a plan! The first step is to research and review all aspects of the project, and produce a clear development program and master business plan defining the services, market, staff, resources and funding required.

The master plan will cover all aspects of the new project and be worded in such a way as to be acceptable to the core group. Clients, staff, volunteers and potential community supporters will need to be inspired by the spiritual potential of the project, whilst suppliers of conventional services and funding will want to be convinced that the project is stable, worthwhile and sustainable. It may require different versions of the master plan with emphasis appropriate to the particular group with which it will be used.

Some members of the core group may feel the expression of their spiritual vision in worldly terms is a betrayal of their fundamental beliefs. This is not so. The need for balance between the spiritual and the material occurs again here. No worthwhile project is brought into being without being grounded in practical terms, and this includes those that are spiritually inspired. Devoted choir monks, spending their life in chanting, prayer and contemplation, were only able to do so in a monastery providing shelter, clothing and food.

The business plan is a living entity and grows and develops as experience is gained throughout the life of the project.

Decision

Up until now, the core group had the exciting task of defining the vision and deciding what was needed for realisation. Eventually comes the point at which a start is needed. A new stage of commitment has been reached. It is tempting to keep putting off this beginning of activity by ever more research and planning, but sooner or later a positive step must be taken. This needs new commitments to volunteers, staff, landlords and suppliers, before the necessary income and financial resources are established. So, this is the vital point where the core group confirms the spiritual inspiration of their objective, and their confidence in its guidance, and makes the decision to start the practical project. They will now need to look at the following:

Funding

It may have been thought that the project will only start when third party funding is available. This will be difficult to achieve. We are studying a spiritually inspired project, not readily understood by conventional sources of funds, and in addition, core funding for administration and staff is anathema to most funders.

Third-party funds will become a possibility once an organisation is established and seen to be delivering useful services. But first it will have to be started, and this will only be possible with support from the core group and their friends. Only modest sums will be required initially, but it may also be necessary to offer personal guarantees to landlords and suppliers of services.

Legal Structure

It might be thought that a not-for-profit organisation, largely run by volunteers, does not need a business structure, but even the smallest project needs to be properly set up and run, if it is to succeed.

The simplest way is to start with an 'Unincorporated Association'. This is an organisation 'Set up through an agreement between a group of people who come together for a reason other than to make a profit'.

It doesn't have to be registered and it doesn't cost anything to set up but needs a formal constitution, recording its members and objects, which banks and other suppliers may want to see. When it starts trading it needs to make an annual tax return.

It is simple to establish, but has the disadvantage that the recorded members are personally responsible for debts and obligations of the association and, as it is not an incorporated body, bank accounts, insurance policies and leases may have to be taken in the personal name of one of the members. This not a problem in the very early days, but is something that needs to be reconsidered once the project grows and the financial sums involved become larger.

Initial steps

Having decided upon the structure, the following action will be necessary:

Premises – An address will be needed for legal purposes and from which the activities are carried out. At first a small rented office or the home of one of the members of the core group will be sufficient.

Name – A distinctive name, not being used by anyone else, will be chosen.

Bank Account – A bank account will be set up and the bank will probably formerly ask for it to be set up in the name of one of the members 'Trading as the Association'.

Presence – A Letterhead, logo, email address, contact telephone number, website, and in due course Facebook page will need to be designed and setup.

Services – The proposed services will be clearly defined and some form of descriptive literature produced.

Staff – Decide upon the people and skills needed to deliver the services and to run the organization. At first, the core group may do all the work.

Publicity – Advertise in some way so that the existence of this new entity is made known to clients, the community and possible supporters.

When the above is complete, the organization exists and is able to start delivering services, albeit on a small scale.

With success will come the need to grow and expand, and this will require the following:

Defining the Service

As the project expands it will be necessary to redefine the nature of the services and terms and costs of delivery.

There is also a need for constant scrutiny of the effectiveness and value of these services. The core group may have been guided to establish the project, only to find potential clients showing little interest. The timing may be inappropriate or the guidance may be planning it as a stepping stone towards something greater. Sensitive attunement is required to ensure that the services are needed – and to make subtle changes as and when necessary.

Value – The core group will understand the spiritual value of the service but the benefits to the community will also have to be made clear.

Statistics – Progress needs to be measured. Potential funders want to see how the service is being used and valued by its customers. A system of recording statistics is necessary in order to supply this information. This information will include numbers and types of clients, services used and financial turnover. This will also be of value to the core group and staff in measuring progress.

Competition – Up-to-date information is needed on what is already available to ensure that the new service is complementary to similar services being supplied by other facilities. It is also important to keep in touch with potentially competing projects in order to maintain a friendly and useful sense of cooperation.

Staff

More people will be needed to run the organisation and deliver the services. The core group decides which tasks they will handle themselves and which will need additional staff. Volunteers will do most of the work but some paid staff may be required.

The selection of suitable staff and volunteers might appear to be a daunting task. But our project is spiritually inspired and guidance is available, not only in defining the tasks but also in inspiring those who are to help, and there will always be people who are already thinking about the concept.

The task is to 'Sound a Clear Note' so that the objects of the project are conveyed in such a way as to obtain a response from people already aware of the idea. This can be done through advertising, talking to individuals, organising a public meeting, etc. As is so often the case in this work, if the project is defined with sufficient clarity, those who do not resonate with the concept will not come forward and wasted conversations will be avoided.

As the project develops, and volunteers, staff and supporters arrive in increasing numbers, a delicate balance will need to be held between the two poles of our dichotomy. There will be those who are spiritually inspired and support the vision but who shy away from what they see as brutal and 'clunky' material plans – and others with the material skills, competence and experience to run the practical side who may despair at the 'fluffy' ideas of their more spiritual colleagues. The task of the core group is to honour and support both poles of this dichotomy and recognize each as being essential for success.

There will be various categories of staff as follows:

Volunteers – Need to be interviewed in order to ascertain whether the person is interested in the project and has the necessary skills, temperament and experience. Although not paid, selected volunteers need a contract in order to avoid misunderstandings in the future. This contract will define their duties and what they may expect from the project.

Paid Staff – Some specialised tasks will require paid staff. As the project grows, someone will have to manage the day-to-day functions. This person may be a volunteer, but it works best with a paid full or part-time manager in this role. With further growth, more administrative tasks such as bookkeeping, website, web sales, packing and despatching will become too much for volunteers to handle, and additional remunerated staff may be necessary.

Professional Advisers – As the work expands, it will be necessary to set up new administrative structures, find larger premises, produce annual accounts and deal with legal contracts. A team of friendly advisers is needed to provide the necessary professional skills and experience.

These professionals will only come on board if they consider the project worthwhile and of value to the community. They may not understand the spiritual side of the services being delivered, and so it will be necessary to stress the more obvious, material benefits. Advisers, convinced of the value of the project, will often give initial information on a non-committal and voluntary basis and only charge where some specific task is called for.

When in doubt about any practical problem, the core group should turn to these advisers. Timely, wise advice will often save a great deal of trouble in the future.

Management Skills – People will be needed with experience in running a business or a project, whether they are amongst the core group, the volunteers, the paid staff or the professional advisors. This experience is needed to set up the internal systems essential if the services are to be delivered in an efficient and sustainable manner.

This is another area where difficulties may be experienced. People, inspired by the spiritual ethos may find themselves reacting to what is a straightforward business problem. It may be a rent review, a demand for a Health and Safety Assessment or some other everyday matter, which appears to have an unhelpful impact on the spiritual project. The organisation needs a way of ensuring practical material decisions are made in a detached and objective fashion, and are not over-influenced by emotional considerations.

Networkers – A vital skill is the ability to make contacts in the community to provide awareness the new project and to develop support. This is a specific talent and if such a person does not exist within the core group or staff, then they need to be found.

Administration

How is the organization to be run and managed? Our projects are similar to conventional businesses, but with differences arising from their spiritually inspired nature. The need for office equipment will be quite straightforward, but there will be some areas where special conditions apply, including:

Planning – Many spiritually inspired people do not take kindly to planning! Their motto is 'go with the flow and let everything effortlessly emerge'. They need to be helped to understand that progress needs a balance between listening to guidance and being open to making changes when necessary, whilst having a clearly defined plan for the practical steps to be taken.

Management Committee – The core group is responsible for policy decisions. As activities increase, it may become necessary to set up a management committee to run the day-to-day activities. This committee will consist of some members of the core group together with others. The number of people in this committee is not critical, but ideally it should be not more than eight, each member being responsible to the committee for a defined range of tasks. The committee is responsible to the core group for administering, managing and supervising all aspects of the services being delivered. They will agree how often they are to meet and how to make decisions.

Many of the responsibilities of this committee are identical with those of a conventional business. However, we are looking at spiritually inspired community projects so that this committee, like the core group, needs to be a peer group. This means there will only be a loose authority structure, and each member will accept the skills of other members and have a clear understanding of how decisions are made.

Again, a delicate balance needs to be held between the spiritual purposes of the project and the practical reality of day-to-day affairs. Walking this particular 'razor's edge' calls for a spirit of sharing and acceptance within the committee.

Officers –- The bank will expect the organisation to have a chair, treasurer and secretary. These officers will be appointed from members of the core group.

Internal Information – Volunteers and staff will be kept informed of progress of the project. They need to feel they are part of an integrated organisation and not just 'cannon fodder' to be deployed at the arbitrary will of the core group. If not handled in a sympathetic manner, there is a risk of the core group being perceived as a small cabal, making decisions imposed on the staff without explanation.

A balance needs to be held as not all members of the staff will understand the spiritual ethos of the project, but all must know the project has a real value and their specific task is a vital part of the whole.

Marketing – Covers all aspects of designing the services and making them known to potential customers. The usual methods are needed including a website, Facebook, Twitter and advertising. Consideration needs to be given to the manner in which the various interests are addressed. Overseas potential clients will need a different approach to that appropriate for local audiences.

Financial Control – Tends to be looked upon as a rather boring area that will look after itself. Once again, as with any conventional business, this will not be the case. Like every other aspect of the project, even though spiritually inspired, the finances need to be grounded in practical reality. This means having a budget, management accounts, cash forecasts, annual accounts and a person to run them and interpret the results that emerge.

Funding

In the early days, the core group used their own resources to pay the small expenses involved. Once the project is started, regular costs will be incurred including rent, rates, telephone and possibly staff. The core group cannot be reasonably expected to carry these increasing costs.

By its nature, the project may not be understood, or even be regarded with suspicion, by funders such as banks and investment trusts. Even if finance is offered, these sources may call for personal guarantees or some form of collateral. It will also be difficult to raise funds from conventional investors, as the project is unlikely to make profits sufficient for it to pay interest or dividends.

If finance cannot be raised from conventional sources, where are these funds to be found? Fortunately, the nature of the project gives it the potential to generate funds from some of its own activities namely:

Sales of Goods or Services – People using the spiritually orientated services may not be able to afford the true cost and it may be necessary to give these free or for a voluntary donation. This can be compensated for by arranging courses, workshops, and talks, compatible with the ethos of the project, but of interest to a wider audience and for which appropriate charges can be made.

A modest income will be generated from these activities but it may well be insufficient to support the whole project and some funds will have to be found from another source.

Patrons and Friends – Conventional sources may find the project difficult to understand, but some people in the community will be in tune with the concept and be potential providers of donations and voluntary help. This friendly support will be vital to make good the short fall in income during the early stages of the project, but in order to get this support, it will be necessary to convince these possible patrons that the project has real value. It is usually best to approach them on a one-to-one basis, but once they are supporting the project, they can be kept in touch with developments by a regular newsletter.

The project has now started and is actively delivering services and supporting itself with the revenue it is generating, but is still at an early stage. In the next chapter, we will in look at how the project matures and grows.

Maturity

The new project is established, staff and volunteers recruited and work has started, now comes the task of delivering the services in an efficient manner. This may feel less stimulating and exciting than the early days of fresh inspiration, but long-term success requires slow and steady growth into maturity. Gentle nursing and support is required in order to reach the point of being firmly established. Apart from the usual needs of a business, special conditions arising from the nature of the project will have to be addressed. These include:

Vision

The start is to visualise the project delivering the services to satisfied customers. The creation of an inspiring vision of the completed project helps to keep positive energy flowing throughout the organisation. For instance, the vision might be to see the project:

'In beautiful, light and airy buildings – with enthusiastic paid staff, abundance of volunteers, necessary equipment and funding all in place.'

As progress is made, conflicting ideas will flow from staff, customers, banks, professional friends and the community at large. Interpreting this information, and acting upon it, requires discernment and the ability to make firm decisions. This in turn means listening to guidance and fine-tuning the vision as necessary.

Sustainability

This is defined as **'the capacity to endure.'** After the first enthusiasm, there may come a time when support fades away. At this stage, methods of sustaining the project in the long-term need to be investigated. This means updating the services to ensure they are relevant and interesting, developing a source of regular income, and being clear how new staff and volunteers will be recruited. Clarity about the long-term sustainability of the venture will become an increasingly important factor in ensuring ongoing enthusiastic support.

Funding

As progress is made, the need for additional finance will begin to loom large. The income generated from the services being delivered to clients, and the wider community, may not be generating sufficient funds to meet the growing costs, and it may still be too early to obtain support from conventional banks and funders – so where to turn?

Income Generator – The next thing to look at is setting up a separate profitable business. Some members of the core group may find it difficult to accept that, for instance, a shop selling conventional objects is appropriate for a spiritual activity, but the project cannot flourish and support its spiritual work, without sufficient reliable funds. Often there will be a way of creating a new business from a slightly altered version of the services already being delivered to the clients of the project.

Conventional Funds – As the project develops, its services will be more widely understood and seen to be serving not only its customers but also the community as a whole. Establishing this understanding opens the way to seek funds from local councils and charitable trusts.

Caution is needed, when considering funds of this nature. They will usually be focused on a particular objective, be short-term, require match funding, and stipulate onerous reporting conditions. Of the total funds required for a particular task, half will have to be found from some other source as match funding, the other half coming from the funder. It is also often found that the additional reporting costs absorb a significant part of the cash supplied by the funder. Such finance is helpful as a one-off, but cannot be relied upon to build a truly sustainable project.

Endowment – When the project is firmly established, credible and sustainable and delivering a worthwhile service to the community at large, it will be in a position to seek endowments. These are gifts granted as an outright donation in the will of a person who believed in the worth of the activity. This is the classic underpinning of the finances of some of the key Glastonbury charities, including the abbey, Chalice Well and the Glastonbury Trust.

Legal Structure

As the level of activity increases, the members of the Association will be exposed to increasing financial risk. At some point it will become advisable to set up a not-for-profit company limited by guarantee. This protects members from the financial perils but has the disadvantage of the higher costs of an annual audit and returns to Companies House.

Careful thought needs to be given as to whether or not to become a registered charity. Being a charity gives tax advantages but with the disadvantage of restricting the objects of the project.

Creativity

As the project grows and develops, the need for holding the balance between practical, material reality and spiritual inspiration will become ever more important, and new opportunities need to be recognised as they arise. The continuing guidance will give subtle hints on possibilities. It will not always be easy to understand these ideas, but no long-term progress will be made without responding to the encouragement and support forthcoming from this source. To make the most of this spiritual inspiration, creativity of every type will be needed including designing projects, copywriting, PR skills, and not least, commercial and entrepreneurial imagination and experience.

As the range of activities expands, the core group needs to be sensitive to the needs of new staff and volunteers, and how they are to be trained and supported.

Support Network

Support of the community at large is a vital component in achieving long-term sustainability. This needs a perception of the project as being worthwhile and useful. Once this is so, there will be a wider interest in attending events, working as volunteers and in making cash donations.

If the services offered are seen to be making a useful contribution to the economy of the town, it may be possible to obtain support from some of the traders. The level of regular donations from supporters is a useful indication of how the community values the project.

Achieving support means providing information on the objects of the project and how they are being achieved. A newsletter, website, and Facebook page will help with this. Building a good relationship with other community projects will also make a positive contribution to the steady growth of activities.

Success and Failure

Any new project will have its ups and downs – moments of triumph and of despair. Through all this, the core group needs to continue in their belief in the project and their ability to achieve final success. Strength and courage will be required to keep going, often in the face of active opposition from others and they will need to constantly reassess the purpose of the project.

> ***If what is trying to emerge is truly honoured,
> then success is assured.***

Success is not necessarily the fulfilment of the original plan. Not every project is able to continue indefinitely in a sustainable and effective fashion. This may necessitate merging with some other venture, reducing the range of services offered or even closing. This might feel like failure, but it is not.

If the project is established in harmony with the original guidance, whatever has been carried out will be useful regardless of the outcome. The core group may wonder why their labours appear to have turned to ashes, but this work will have set the foundation upon which a future project can be built, with less expenditure of energy than would otherwise be necessary.

A typical pattern seen over and over again in community projects is a start being made with great enthusiasm by the inspired initiators. The activity may go from strength to strength in the early days, but often moves into a second stage, where no forward progress appears to be made, but it keeps going in a rather unexciting and plodding fashion.

This middle period often lasts for many years. If the project is destined to come into being, there comes a moment when the time is right, new people arrive with enthusiasm, and the project is taken forward into next stage of its growth. Those caring for it during this 'marking time' period have maintained a firm platform upon which, in time, new energy can build and grow. This process of moving in surges of activity and periods of tranquillity – a sort of staircase – is often seen. It is necessary to recognise these quiet interim period as making a positive contribution to the ultimate fulfilling of the vision.

Keep Going

It is vital that all concerned believe in the value and achievability of the objectives. Hearts are bound to falter, but this key belief will help the project to survive when all seems too difficult. Holding a clear vision of how it will feel when the project is up and flying will ensure final success.

With true guidance, accompanied by love and dedication, sooner or later the spiritual objective will be achieved.

There are no failures with these projects – only steps upon the way to realising the ultimate vision.

We are nearing the end of our journey but need to look at one last subject – the unique problems experienced when working with these projects.

Apparent 'Problems'

We will now explore the obstructions to sustainable growth experienced by spiritually inspired projects. All new ventures encounter difficulties but some unusual factors affect those in which we are interested. In these cases the apparent trials are not only opportunities for growth, but are part of a 'winnowing process,' which allows successful projects to flourish and unsuitable ones to wither and die. Some of these problems are given below in alphabetical order

Balance

We described earlier the characteristics required in core group, staff and volunteers, Lack of these qualities will leave an opening for uncertainty to creep in resulting in a weakening of the intent of the project. Some special problems arise when holding the balance in groups committed to spiritual projects and some of these are as follows:

Authority – The core group, in particular, consists of peers – a group with equal authority but with different skills. This is perfection, but as we are dealing with real live human beings, there will inevitably be a difference in natural charisma and authority; hence the importance of every individual having the strength and courage to speak openly to a member who is endeavouring to dominate the group, and being fully supported in so doing.

Compassion – Spiritual projects hold a balance between two opposing forces. The mystical vision, carried out in a loving and caring way, matched with practical material efficiency.

Some may think kindness is needed at all times and no-one's feelings should ever be hurt. Others may feel that being over compassionate gets in the way of essential practical decisions. Such differences will inevitably occur. If not addressed, they lead to resentment and undercurrents of unspoken emotional tension. If something is not working, the problem needs to be tackled in a straightforward but compassionate and gentle fashion. This may require talking through painful personal matters, but avoiding the situation will lead to more damage than facing it with courage.

Delegation – A source of potential problems lies in individuals, inspired by the project but having little or no experience of managing staff. As a result, a person may create and develop a specific service and feel that only he can look after every detail to ensure success. There must be continual vigilance to ensure that when a service is developing rapidly, a sufficient number of people are involved to ensure proper delivery, and that each is empowered to take responsibility for a specific part. Only by effective delegation, can the project flourish.

Intent – The organisation needs to be both inspired spiritually and managed in an efficient manner. There will be an on-going tendency to move towards either a more 'floating' spirituality or a more 'concrete' materialism. This needs to be watched, as a strong movement towards either of these poles will damage the project.

Skills – the staff and volunteers must contain all the skills and experience needed. If any are missing, they need to be found from friendly, outside support. There is a tendency to think existing members of the team can cope with any situation. This blindness to weakness and lack is a serious vulnerability.

Distraction

There is a continuing pressure of mundane, but essential, details, which can lead to losing the broad vision and understanding of the true purpose of the project. The key to success for all community projects is constant attention and commitment to the originating vision, and overcoming the distraction of everyday details as part of the process.

Entropy

Entropy is a term used in thermodynamics to describe the way in which structures gradually decline into disorder unless maintained by a continual input of energy.

This also applies to human activities. A huge amount of effort is put into establishing and building a project, but without the contribution of continuing inspiration and work, it will gradually lose energy and may even disintegrate and disappear.

In Glastonbury, entropy is ever present. Apparent 'Forces of Chaos' resent any attempt to build a new structure and do their best to destroy the activity. The effects of these 'negative' forces seem to be more powerful than would be expected from simple tiredness and boredom of those running the project.

Confusion of purpose appears to be the characteristic that opens the door for chaos to enter, and it does so where any lack of clarity between individuals is found.

The answer is 'clarity of contract', in legal, written and verbal agreements. This necessitates all parties being clear about the understanding reached and being prepared to honour this as far as possible. If it is necessary to change something, then all parties must agree. Any departure from this clarity will open the way for the forces of chaos to make merry – and they are very good at this!

Lack of clarity of obligations is a frequent cause of the failure of community projects. Uncertainty leaves a vacuum for the ever-present forces of chaos to enter in the form of malicious gossip, rumours and misunderstandings, all of which serve to undermine the clarity of purpose of the venture.

In addition to the dangers of confusion is the slow decline of the project due to lack of continuing input of inspiring energy. A time may come when the initiators feel they have had enough and hand over to others. In some cases, those who take over will enjoy running the project but be unable or unwilling to contribute the initiative; inspiration and energy needed keep the organization progressing towards its full potential.

The forces of entropy are overcome with clarity of contract, inspired vision and continuing energy invested in the project.

These negative energies have a positive part to play in that they bring to bear a cleansing and sieving process. If the concept is not inspired, understood and attuned with the purposes of Glastonbury, then the over-lighting energy will do its best to prevent the activity from flourishing.

Fragmentation

There is an expression in astrology called the 'Precession of the Equinoxes' and in astronomy 'Axial Precession'. This is the phenomenon whereby the Earth's axis appears to move in an anticlockwise direction against the fixed stars taking some 26,000 years to complete a circuit. Astrology allocates 12 signs of the Zodiac to specific constellations in the night sky. The earth's axis moved through the sign of Pisces from A.D. 0 to around A.D. 2000, when it entered the sign of Aquarius, where it will remain for another 2000 years. The transit from sign to sign is a slow process and takes place over many years, but this is the broad pattern. Astrology calls these two phases the Age of Pisces and the Age of Aquarius.

Astrology claims that the Piscean Age was one of authority and control – strong leaders deciding how people should live and compliant individuals going along with what they were told. We are now entering the Aquarian Age with which comes the emergence of strong feelings of individuality. People want to look after their own lives, make their own choices and are suspicious of authority. This has led to democracy, but also the increasing difficulty of running a project, not to mention a country. This difficulty comes particularly into focus in Glastonbury.

Many of those involved in starting new community projects in Glastonbury have been 'called to serve' in the town. Often, a high price has been paid in honouring this call; jobs, families, partners and friends have been left behind. Whilst the way of living is enjoyed, there is often a reluctance to impair this new freedom by making the compromises that would be required to work with others.

A development resulting from this individuality is the way in which different projects flourish and thrive. Individuals concentrate upon the project with which they feel inspired, and pour their energy into making it a success. With this seems to go an 'inward looking' and reluctance to understand and work with other projects.

Our thesis is that these apparent problems eventually make a positive contribution to the emergence of the real purpose of the town. How does this materialize in this case?

Positive results have been achieved in the way in which various individual projects are thriving. This seems to have been a necessary process in helping the Whole to flourish. With the emerging realisation of the success of the components has come an awareness of the need for closer cooperation. This in turn brings an awareness of a need for clarity of vision, not only of the individual projects, which we described above, but of the town as a whole. Perhaps this would not be so clear if the individual projects had not emerged so strongly.

Poverty Consciousness

This is a particular problem found in Glastonbury arising from the concept that no charge should be made for spiritual services, coupled with the idea that true servants of the spirit are devoted to poverty.

The monks of old understood that delivering a spiritually inspired service required a balanced material life. 'The labourer is worthy of his hire' and every individual deserves sufficient personal income to enable him to carry out the work he is called to do. Understanding this concept leads to the realisation that income needs to be generated from possibly mundane tasks in order to support unpaid spiritual work.

Premises

Suitable premises are the key to success of any project. In the early days there may be insufficient income to pay rent and rates on premises, and certainly not enough to purchase a property. But the existence of physical space to enable the services to be delivered helps the energy to build and people to become involved.

Creating Spirituality Inspired Projects - Apparent 'Problems'

So a high priority is to be given to acquiring a place from which to operate. This may initially be rented but will need to be owned to ensure long-term sustainability. This requires substantial funding and securing these funds is an essential part of the business plan. The problem of acquiring suitable premises is one of the imperatives that drive the project forward.

Sensitivity

This is needed in the interests of the community. Working in harmony with the community as a whole is essential but not always easy. Sensitivity is also needed to the group running the project. Sustaining a harmonious working group is not always easy. Personality clashes and differences of opinions will occur and need to be treated with sensitivity and firmness, if they are not to damage the work of the group.

Talents

Glastonbury is blessed with many talented people, 'called' to live in the town, including artists, musicians, writers, therapists, and computer experts. More graduates are to be found here than in most small towns.

At the moment, this wealth of talent tends to be under-employed. Generating a reasonable income in Glastonbury is not easy and many bright people are working behind shop counters and doing other pedestrian jobs. Such tasks are valuable and rewarding in themselves, but a more appropriate use of these skills would provide a better income and help the town as a whole to flourish.

This is another possible 'cloud with a silver lining'. People are drawn to the town, and may mistakenly think this will enable them to blossom in doing something entirely different to that which they followed in the outside world. Glastonbury does indeed need the inherent talents of the people that it calls, but it also requires the practical skills they have developed and honed in their professional life. The difficulties experienced in finding worthwhile work will help them to understand the need for balance between their inherent talents and their materially honed skills. It may well be that they are being asked to do something very similar to that which they did before they came to Glastonbury, but this time using this experience in a project that is spiritually inspired.

Once this understanding is reached, their true niche in the town will become clear and lead to achieving a personal balance between adequate income and an enjoyable and fulfilling place in the community.

Vision

Nothing can be successfully started without a clear vision. In our case, the original 'inspired one' accesses what we call the 'over-lighting energy' of Glastonbury, 'attunes' with what is being called for, and puts into writing a plan of the objective.

What is required is obvious, but keeping in touch with this intent is not always easy. Once the project starts, a whole welter of new difficulties will arise, involving cash flow, volunteers, people, equipment and other resources. Such practical details tend to cause confusion and distraction unless a conscious effort is made to keep reaffirming the original vision in the certainty of achievement.

The Positive Aspect to Problems

The apparent difficulties we have listed, in fact, make a positive contribution to the success of the project by compelling constant attention to the clarity of vision and sharing this with all involved.

A clear and consistent pattern emerges:

Apparently negative influences tend to disrupt everything we set out to do but these forces play a constructive role in compelling us to focus with clarity on what we are trying to achieve.

Conclusion

We have finished our exploration of spiritually inspired projects with a peripheral investigation of the world of the spirit and its effect on our subject. I will end with a summary of the more important aspects.

As with any business or charity, for success these projects need to be soundly financed and well managed.

Inspired individuals are needed who accept the presence of a divine plan, who listen to the available guidance throughout the life of the project, and are willing to take the action necessary to start the activity and to inspire those willing to help.

These individuals form a core group, draw up a plan for materialising the original idea and promote the concept with such clarity that others respond and come forward to help. This vivid vision creates around it an 'Aura' of protection. In moments of crisis, as if by magic, the right people arrive with offers of help and the needed resources materialise in unexpected ways.

With clarity of purpose, go the qualities of openness, honesty and integrity. Any deviousness will at some time come to light and damage the project. This applies both to day-to-day personal relations and also business undertakings and agreements.

To flourish, the activity needs the energy and support of people with a range of skills. Sensitivity is needed in allowing supporters to provide their experience so that they find enjoyment and fulfilment whilst contributing to the success of the venture.

Individuals do not own these organizations but many will feel personally involved. The primary purpose is to deliver a useful service rather than being a vehicle for personal recognition and care is needed to ensure feelings of ownership do not creep in. Awareness is also needed in recognizing and resolving normal, human, emotional dramas in a calm and compassionate fashion.

A time will come when those who initiated the project need to move on. An established organization has a life of its own and persists as long as inspiration continues and it is managed with love and efficiency. When retiring, those who have been 'stewards', and held responsibility, need to help find people with the right intent to be their successors.

Apparent problems may be ways of fine-tuning and improving the organisation. If these difficulties are seen as potential opportunities and lessons, what appear to be obstructions, can be transformed into positive help in achieving the objectives.

Distraction is easy with projects of this nature. They are started with divine inspiration, but before long can be bogged down in negotiations with the local council about a business-rating bill. Vigilance is needed in order to float without effort through essential material duties whilst holding the vision of the ultimate objective. An esoteric saying is:

'Keep your eyes on the mountain top
whilst not to tripping over the stones at your feet.'

Another aspect is awareness of balance – to 'Walk the Razor's Edge'. Over and over again, we come across dichotomies to be honoured and held in harmony between:

Creating Spirituality Inspired Projects – Conclusion

- Divine inspiration and material needs.

- Loving kindness and practical reality.

- The desire for perceived success and the spiritual needs of the project.

- Praise of personal achievements and the reality of the divine task.

- The wish for abundance of cash flowing through the project and the need to manage on limited resources.

Balance is called for at almost every stage and 'walking this tightrope' contributes many lessons.

Our discussions may make the creation of spiritually inspired projects sound difficult – and indeed hard work is involved – but there are compensations. Service, in harmony with divine inspiration, brings a sense of effortless flow, joy, companionship and personal fulfilment.

The emphasis in this book is on work in Glastonbury in England. Experience gained here will be applicable to any other place where an inspiring spiritual presence has a clear idea of what it is trying to achieve, and where there are individuals able to respond to this vision.

I hope the lessons gained here will be of value to others, wherever they may be.

APPENDICES

Appendix1 - Wisdom

The wisdom is a vast subject covering all aspects of human life and we touched on some of these characteristics in an earlier chapter. Below is a list of other aspects that the reader might like to explore further. We give these items in alphabetical order rather than importance or significance.

Abundance

The divine is unlimited, with enough for all and no shortages. This abundance is released through positive visualisation, directed towards the un-manifest energy of the etheric plane, which is capable of generating limitless material wealth and artefacts. Thoughts of lack and poverty consciousness result in a restriction in the flow of plenty. The individual is responsible for using his skills, talents and intuition to create the affluence appropriate to the community in which he lives.

Action

A fulfilled spiritual life requires a delicate balance between 'being' and 'acting'. Being is necessary in order to attune with the cosmos and receive the energy and guidance available. Being on its own is not enough – the fruits need to be realised in Action in the World for the benefit of all.

Attraction

Attraction is a fundamental law, flowing from the Wisdom and found in all religions and faiths: 'Like attracts like'. Positive thoughts produce positive results, negative thoughts the opposite. An optimistic attitude creates a constructive outcome. This rule applies to both material and spiritual activities.

Between Incarnations

At the end of each incarnation, the incarnated being dies. The physical body is left behind whilst the spirit moves on to the spiritual world. No Angel stands at the Gates of Heaven, approving entry, but what is expected is found – if Jesus is anticipated, he will be waiting, if someone else, then she or he will be found. The dying one is always welcomed by friendly and loving beings, some of whom may be relatives or old friends.

The period between lives is used to recollect and meditate upon lessons learnt in the one recently completed. This interim period is described in detail in the Egyptian and Tibetan Buddhist 'Books of the Dead'. Negative deeds are brought into painful and clear perspective whilst those of a positive nature are understood and valued.

With completion of this process comes the time for a new life. With the help and guidance of advanced spirits, a decision is made upon where this is to be and into which family the seller is to be born. This choice is based upon what the soul needs to learn and experience in continuing its journey.

Discipline

Wisdom defines discipline as an integral part of the spiritual life. This includes a simple and regular routine, bodily cleanliness and abstention from alcohol and other drugs.

Discrimination

Everything is in a process of transition. The only unchanging One is the divine and the only eternal component of the individual is the spirit. Discrimination is needed to remain focussed on the eternal Wisdom when surrounded by the activities and emotional disturbances of the ever-changing material world. This same discernment is needed when deciding the role of service and in guarding against the ever-present desire to control people and events.

Evil

Evil is one of the questions addressed by every religion. If God is omniscient, infinite, eternal, and embraces all, then this must include what appears to be evil. Wisdom teaching tends to look at evil as absence of the good. This comes about through humans deciding to follow a negative rather than a positive path.

Some of the established religions see evil as a personality fighting the good. The mystic, Rudolf Steiner, offered an interesting interpretation. He claimed human evolution is held in balance between the good, which he called the cosmic Christ, and two evil entities:

The Light Spirit – Lucifer motivates creativity and spirituality, but with a negative aspect in tempting human pride with the delusion of divinity.

The Dark Spirit – Ahriman stimulates intellectuality and technology, but has a negative influence when encouraging humans to live on the material plane and whilst denying their oneness with the divine.

Faith

A belief in the world of the Spirit is necessary in order to walk the spiritual path. Without this faith, even the first step cannot be taken. Initially, it may be difficult to accept this concept – an effective start is to work on this as a hypothesis, then to carry out a spiritual practice from which acceptable experiential proof will emerge.

Faithfulness

In spite of the inevitable desert periods and 'Dark Nights of the Soul', continued faithfulness to the intuition and guidance is called for.

Flexibility

The task we have been given may subtly change as we progress. Listening to hints received, and making changes as new circumstances dictate, is a necessary part of working in this way.

Gratitude

Showing gratitude for all flowing into our life encourages and enhances a positive attitude even when illness and adverse conditions are experienced.

Humility

This is not the same as meekness but a willingness to serve without seeking personal recognition or acclaim. Pride is a natural and understandable emotion but becomes one of the greatest dangers on the path when invested in personal achievement, whether spiritual or material.

Humility is often learned, in a painful fashion, through the experience of an apparent disastrous failure in an area where we felt proud of our prowess.

Initiation

The completion of a stage on the spiritual path is marked by initiation. The individual then moves on to make further progress. The initiatory phases are defined in most Mystery Schools.

Love

The essence of the Wisdom is the view of the cosmos being created and held together through the power of divine love – a wise, compassionate, detached love and quite different to the emotional, selfish and possessive love found in human affairs. The developing an awareness of universal compassion, and unattached love for all beings, is key task on the journey.

Motive

The objective may be growing closer to the divine, serving in the community or building a physical bridge. Whatever the object, the purity of motive lying behind the purpose is what matters.

Practice

A regular spiritual practice is necessary. This is a disciplined method of contacting the divine, whether by prayer, contemplation, meditation or one of many other exercises.

A widely performed practice is that of meditation. This involves sitting in a private place for 20 or 30 minutes and using some method to still what the Hindus call the ever active 'monkey mind'. Many methods are available but the most common are watching the breath or saying a mantra, a repeated phrase or word, which may or may not have a meaning. This is wide spread throughout the Eastern religions and is well recognized in the Jesus prayer used, by the Orthodox Eastern Christian Church – 'Lord Jesus Christ, son of God, have mercy on me'.

Thought

The Wisdom states:

'Energy follows thought' – as you think so shall you be.'

What is held in the mind is created. This applies not only to personal characteristics but also to practical achievements.

Transformation

The individual needs to be transformed from the original Earth-bound physical human into a new form of spiritual being. This transformative process takes place by the conscientious following of the tenets of the path. Many religions talk about being 'born again' or 'reborn'. This means leaving the old material way of living and starting anew with an emphasis on the call of the spirit.

Appendix 2 - Glastonbury

Books

'A Pilgrim in Glastonbury', my previous book, is available on Amazon and contains information about Glastonbury and some of the spiritually inspired projects to be found in this town.

It also contains a bibliography of books on spirituality and Glastonbury.

Websites

The following are Glastonbury websites giving a wealth of information on the town.

www.glastonbury.co.uk – providing comprehensive information for visitors and residents listing services including accommodation, shops, how to get there and community projects.

www.glastonburyoracle.co.uk – giving details of what's on, events, venues and services.

www.unitythroughdiversity.org – activities of the Glastonbury Pilgrim Reception Centre and other community projects.

Creating Spirituality Inspired Projects

www.ingramcontent.com/pod-product-compliance
Lightning Source LLC
Chambersburg PA
CBHW020438220526
45464CB00002B/755